*Promises for You*

# Promises for You
## from the New International Version

previously published as

### God's Promises for You from the New International Version

*Compiled by Christopher D. Hudson
and Lindsay Vanker*

inspirio
*The gift group of Zondervan*

# Table of Contents

# Foreword

*by Joni Eareckson Tada*

*In the beginning was the Word, and the Word was*
*with God, and the Word was God.—John 1:1*

The Bible reveals God's soul to us in a way that no
other book is able to do. It is history, wisdom, and
poetry. It is unparalleled as a compendium of theology, philosophy, and ethics. It is a gospel tract, distilling the essence of our relationship of an eternal God.

Though the Bible contains all these things, it is at
its heart an autobiography. The Bible is all about
God. Through even the most twisted and unlikely
narratives, some even tawdry, we see God's soul
reflected to us.

Every word speaks something to us of his soul.

Treasure God's Word today. In everything you
read, you will come to know the soul of God, he who
is the lover of your soul.

# Plan of Salvation

*by Billy Graham*

The Bible says that we have been separated and alien-
ated from God because we have willfully turned our
backs on Him and are determined to run our lives
without Him. This is what the Bible means by *sin*—
choosing our way instead of God's way, and not giving Him His rightful place in our lives. The evidence
of this is all around us, in the moral chaos and
heartache of our world. The headlines scream every
day that we live in a broken, sin-ravaged world.

But in addition, the message declares that God still
loves us. He yearns to forgive us and bring us back to
Himself. He wants to fill our lives with meaning and
purpose right now. Then He wants us to spend all
eternity with Him in Heaven, free forever from the
pain and sorrow and death of this world.

Moreover, God has done everything possible to
reconcile us to Himself. He did this in a way that
staggers our imagination. In God's plan, by His death
on the Cross, Jesus Christ paid the penalty for our
sins, taking the judgment of God that we deserve
upon Himself when He died on the Cross. Now, by
His resurrection from the dead, Christ has broken the

bonds of death and opened the way to eternal life
for us.

The resurrection also confirms for all time that
Jesus was in fact who He said He was: the unique Son
of God, sent from Heaven to save us from our sins.
Now God freely offers us the gift of forgiveness and
eternal life.

Finally, this message is about our response. Like
any other gift, God's gift of salvation does not become
ours until we accept it and make it our own. God has
done everything possible to provide salvation. But we
must reach out in faith and accept it.

How do we do this?

First, by confessing to God that we are sinners and
in need of His forgiveness; then by repenting of our
sins and, with God's help, turning from them.

Second, by committing our lives to Jesus Christ as
Lord and Savior. The best-known verse in the New
Testament states the Gospel concisely: "For God so
loved the world that he gave his one and only Son,
that whoever believes in him shall not perish but have
eternal life. For God did not send his Son into the
world to condemn the world, but to save the world
through him" (John 3:16-17). God in His grace
invites us to receive His Son into our lives today.

If you have never done so, I invite you to bow your head right now and by a simple prayer of faith open your heart to Jesus Christ. God receives us just as we are. No matter who we are or what we have done, we are saved only because of what Christ has done for us. . I will not go to Heaven because I have preached to great crowds. I will go to Heaven for one reason: Jesus Christ died for me, and I am trusting Him alone for my salvation. Christ died for you also, and He freely offers you the gift of eternal life as you commit your life to Him.

When you do, you become a child of God, adopted into His family forever. He also comes to live within you and will begin to change you from within. No one who truly gives his or her life to Christ will ever be the same, for the promise of His Word is true: "Therefore, if anyone is in Christ, he is a new creation; the old has gone, the new has come! All this is from God, who reconciled us to himself through Christ and gave us the ministry of reconciliation" (2 Corinthians 5:17-18).

We have seen this happen countless times all over the world, and it can happen in your life as well. Open your life to Christ today.

*Promises for you*

# Acceptance

**JOHN 6:37**
All that the Father gives me will come to me, and whoever comes to me I will never drive away.

**1 TIMOTHY 2:3-4**
This is good, and pleases God our Savior, who wants all men to be saved and to come to a knowledge of the truth.

**ROMANS 15:7**
Accept one another, then, just as Christ accepted you, in order to bring praise to God.

**LUKE 15:6-7**
Then [the shepherd] calls his friends and neighbors together and says, "Rejoice with me; I have found my lost sheep." I tell you that in the same way there will be more rejoicing in heaven over one sinner who repents than over ninety-nine righteous persons who do not need to repent.

## 1 TIMOTHY 4:9-10

This is a trustworthy saying that deserves full acceptance (and for this we labor and strive), that we have put our hope in the living God, who is the Savior of all men, and especially of those who believe.

## JAMES 2:2-4

Suppose a man comes into your meeting wearing a gold ring and fine clothes, and a poor man in shabby clothes also comes in. If you show special attention to the man wearing fine clothes and say, "Here's a good seat for you," but say to the poor man, "You stand there" or "Sit on the floor by my feet," have you not discriminated among yourselves and become judges with evil thoughts?

## ROMANS 14:1

Accept him whose faith is weak, without passing judgment on disputable matters.

## MATTHEW 7:2

For in the same way you judge others, you will be judged, and with the measure you use, it will be measured to you.

# Armor of God

**2 CORINTHIANS 10:4**
The weapons we fight with are not the weapons of the world. On the contrary, they have divine power to demolish strongholds.

**EPHESIANS 6:11**
Put on the full armor of God so that you can take your stand against the devil's schemes.

**ROMANS 13:12**
The night is nearly over; the day is almost here. So let us put aside the deeds of darkness and put on the armor of light.

**1 THESSALONIANS 5:8**
But since we belong to the day, let us be self-controlled, putting on faith and love as a breastplate, and the hope of salvation as a helmet.

**EPHESIANS 6:17**
Take the helmet of salvation and the sword of the
Spirit, which is the word of God.

**COLOSSIANS 3:12**
As God's chosen people, holy and dearly loved, clothe
yourselves with compassion, kindness, humility, gentleness and patience.

**HEBREWS 4:12**
For the word of God is living and active. Sharper
than any double-edged sword, it penetrates even to
dividing soul and spirit, joints and marrow; it judges
the thoughts and attitudes of the heart.

**1 PETER 5:5**
Young men, in the same way be submissive to those
who are older. All of you, clothe yourselves with
humility toward one another, because,

> "God opposes the proud
> but gives grace to the humble."

# Assurance

**HEBREWS 11:1**
Now faith is being sure of what we hope for and
certain of what we do not see.

**ROMANS 8:38-39**
For I am convinced that neither death nor life,
neither angels nor demons, neither the present nor
the future, nor any powers, neither height nor depth,
nor anything else in all creation, will be able to separate us from the love of God that is in Christ Jesus
our Lord.

**ISAIAH 54:10**
"Though the mountains be shaken
    and the hills be removed,
yet my unfailing love for you will not be shaken
    nor my covenant of peace be removed,"
says the LORD, who has compassion on you.

**JOHN 10:27-29**
My sheep listen to my voice; I know them, and they
follow me. I give them eternal life, and they shall
never perish; no one can snatch them out of my

hand. My Father, who has given them to me, is greater than all; no one can snatch them out of my Father's hand.

### 1 TIMOTHY 3:13

Those who have served well gain an excellent standing and great assurance in their faith in Christ Jesus.

### 2 TIMOTHY 1:12

I am not ashamed, because I know whom I have believed, and am convinced that he is able to guard what I have entrusted to him for that day.

### HEBREWS 10:19, 22

Brothers, since we have confidence to enter the Most Holy Place by the blood of Jesus ... let us draw near to God with a sincere heart in full assurance of faith, having our hearts sprinkled to cleanse us from a guilty conscience and having our bodies washed with pure water.

### 1 JOHN 5:14-15

This is the confidence we have in approaching God: that if we ask anything according to his will, he hears us. And if we know that he hears us—whatever we ask—we know that we have what we asked of him.

# Atonement

**1 JOHN 4:10**
This is love: not that we loved God, but that he
loved us and sent his Son as an atoning sacrifice for
our sins.

**COLOSSIANS 1:19-20**
For God was pleased to have all his fullness dwell in
him, and through him to reconcile to himself all
things, whether things on earth or things in heaven,
by making peace through his blood, shed on the
cross.

**MATTHEW 26:28**
This is my blood of the covenant, which is poured
out for many for the forgiveness of sins.

**COLOSSIANS 2:13-14**
When you were dead in your sins and in the uncircumcision of your sinful nature, God made you alive
with Christ. He forgave us all our sins, having canceled the written code, with its regulations, that was

against us and that stood opposed to us; he took it
away, nailing it to the cross.

### 1 JOHN 2:2
He is the atoning sacrifice for our sins, and not only
for ours but also for the sins of the whole world.

### 1 PETER 1:18-19
For you know that it was not with perishable things
such as silver or gold that you were redeemed from
the empty way of life handed down to you from your
forefathers, but with the precious blood of Christ, a
lamb without blemish or defect.

### ROMANS 5:9
Since we have now been justified by his blood, how
much more shall we be saved from God's wrath
through him!

### HEBREWS 9:28
Christ was sacrificed once to take away the sins of
many people; and he will appear a second time, not
to bear sin, but to bring salvation to those who are
waiting for him.

# Belief

## JOHN 3:16

For God so loved the world that he gave his one and only Son, that whoever believes in him shall not perish but have eternal life.

## JOHN 6:47

I tell you the truth, he who believes has everlasting life.

## ROMANS 10:9-10

If you confess with your mouth, "Jesus is Lord," and believe in your heart that God raised him from the dead, you will be saved. For it is with your heart that you believe and are justified, and it is with your mouth that you confess and are saved.

## JOHN 11:25-26

Jesus said to her, "I am the resurrection and the life. He who believes in me will live, even though he dies; and whoever lives and believes in me will never die. Do you believe this?"

**ACTS 16:31**
They replied, "Believe in the Lord Jesus, and you will be saved—you and your household."

**JOHN 3:18**
Whoever believes in him is not condemned.

**ACTS 10:43**
All the prophets testify about him that everyone who believes in him receives forgiveness of sins through his name.

**JOHN 1:12**
To all who received him, to those who believed in his name, he gave the right to become children of God.

**JOHN 20:29**
Jesus told him, "Because you have seen me, you have believed; blessed are those who have not seen and yet have believed."

**HEBREWS 11:6**
Without faith it is impossible to please God, because anyone who comes to him must believe that he exists and that he rewards those who earnestly seek him.

# Blessings

**PSALM 1:1-2**

Blessed is the man
    who does not walk in the counsel of the wicked
or stand in the way of sinners
    . or sit in the seat of mockers.
But his delight is in the law of the LORD,
    and on his law he meditates day and night.

**JEREMIAH 17:7**

Blessed is the man who trusts in the LORD,
whose confidence is in him.

**EPHESIANS 1:3**

Praise be to the God and Father of our Lord Jesus
Christ, who has blessed us in the heavenly realms
with every spiritual blessing in Christ.

**PSALM 31:19**

How great is your goodness,
    which you have stored up for those who fear
        you,

which you bestow in the sight of men
on those who take refuge in you.

**JOHN 1:16**
From the fullness of his grace we have all received one
blessing after another.

**PSALM 103:2-3**
Praise the LORD, O my soul,
and forget not all his benefits—
who forgives all your sins
and heals all your diseases.

**ROMANS 10:12-13**
For there is no difference between Jew and Gentile—
the same Lord is Lord of all and richly blesses all who
call on him, for, "Everyone who calls on the name of
the Lord will be saved."

**JAMES 1:17**
Every good and perfect gift is from above, coming
down from the Father of the heavenly lights, who
does not change like shifting shadows.

**PSALM 16:11**

You have made known to me the path of life;
> you will fill me with joy in your presence,
with eternal pleasures at your right hand.

**PSALM 65:4**

Blessed are those you choose
> and bring near to live in your courts!
We are filled with the good things of your house,
> of your holy temple.

**JEREMIAH 31:14**

"I will satisfy the priests with abundance,
> and my people will be filled with my bounty,"
declares the LORD.

**EZEKIEL 34:26-27**

I will bless them and the places surrounding my hill. I
will send down showers in season; there will be showers of blessing. The trees of the field will yield their
fruit and the ground will yield its crops; the people
will be secure in their land. They will know that I am
the LORD, when I break the bars of their yoke and
rescue them from the hands of those who enslaved
them.

**MALACHI 3:10**

"Bring the whole tithe into the storehouse, that there may be food in my house. Test me in this," says the LORD Almighty, "and see if I will not throw open the floodgates of heaven and pour out so much blessing that you will not have room enough for it."

**DEUTERONOMY 11:26-27**

See, I am setting before you today a blessing and a curse—the blessing if you obey the commands of the LORD your God that I am giving you today.

**GENESIS 12:2-3**

I will make you into a great nation
   and I will bless you;
I will make your name great,
   and you will be a blessing.
I will bless those who bless you,
   and whoever curses you I will curse;
and all peoples on earth
   will be blessed through you.

**MATTHEW 5:3**

Blessed are the poor in spirit,
               for theirs is the kingdom of heaven.

# Boldness

## HEBREWS 10:23
Let us hold unswervingly to the hope we profess, for he who promised is faithful.

## ROMANS 1:16
I am not ashamed of the gospel, because it is the power of God for the salvation of everyone who believes: first for the Jew, then for the Gentile.

## PHILIPPIANS 1:20
I eagerly expect and hope that I will in no way be ashamed, but will have sufficient courage so that now as always Christ will be exalted in my body, whether by life or by death.

## 2 TIMOTHY 1:12
I am not ashamed, because I know whom I have believed, and am convinced that he is able to guard what I have entrusted to him for that day.

## PSALM 27:1

The LORD is my light and my salvation—
    whom shall I fear?
The LORD is the stronghold of my life—
    of whom shall I be afraid?

## ROMANS 8:31-32

If God is for us, who can be against us? He who did
not spare his own Son, but gave him up for us all—
how will he not also, along with him, graciously give
us all things?

## DEUTERONOMY 31:6

Be strong and courageous. Do not be afraid or terri-
fied because of them, for the LORD your God goes
with you; he will never leave you nor forsake you.

## PSALM 27:14

Wait for the LORD;
    be strong and take heart
    and wait for the LORD.

## ISAIAH 40:29

He gives strength to the weary
    and increases the power of the weak.

# Celebration

**ISAIAH 61:10**

I delight greatly in the LORD;
    my soul rejoices in my God.
For he has clothed me with garments of salvation
    and arrayed me in a robe of righteousness,
as a bridegroom adorns his head like a priest,
    and as a bride adorns herself with her jewels.

**PSALM 30:11-12**

You turned my wailing into dancing;
    you removed my sackcloth and clothed me
        with joy,
that my heart may sing to you and not be silent.
    O LORD my God, I will give you thanks forever.

**PSALM 149:3**

Let them praise his name with dancing
    and make music to him with tambourine
        and harp.

**ISAIAH 12:6**

Shout aloud and sing for joy, people of Zion,
    for great is the Holy One of Israel among you.

ZEPHANIAH 3:17
> The LORD your God is with you,
>> he is mighty to save.
> He will take great delight in you,
>> he will quiet you with his love,
>> he will rejoice over you with singing.

EXODUS 15:2
> The LORD is my strength and my song;
>> he has become my salvation.
> He is my God, and I will praise him,
>> my father's God, and I will exalt him.

PSALM 47:1-2
> Clap your hands, all you nations;
>> shout to God with cries of joy.
> How awesome is the LORD Most High,
> the great King over all the earth!

ISAIAH 65:18-19
> Be glad and rejoice forever
>> in what I will create,
> for I will create Jerusalem to be a delight
>> and its people a joy.
> I will rejoice over Jerusalem
>> and take delight in my people;
> the sound of weeping and of crying
>> will be heard in it no more.

# Character

**JAMES 3:13**
Who is wise and understanding among you? Let him show it by his good life, by deeds done in the humility that comes from wisdom.

**1 TIMOTHY 4:12**
Set an example for the believers in speech, in life, in love, in faith and in purity.

**ROMANS 12:17**
Be careful to do what is right in the eyes of everybody.

**TITUS 3:1**
Remind the people to be subject to rulers and authorities, to be obedient, to be ready to do whatever is good.

**PROVERBS 13:6**
Righteousness guards the man of integrity,
but wickedness overthrows the sinner.

## PSALM 84:11

For the LORD God is a sun and shield;
the LORD bestows favor and honor;
no good thing does he withhold
from those whose walk is blameless.

## JOB 17:9

The righteous will hold to their ways,
and those with clean hands will grow stronger.

## LUKE 16:10

Whoever can be trusted with very little can also be
trusted with much, and whoever is dishonest with
very little will also be dishonest with much.

## 2 CORINTHIANS 1:12

Now this is our boast: Our conscience testifies that
we have conducted ourselves in the world, and especially in our relations with you, in the holiness and
sincerity that are from God. We have done so not
according to worldly wisdom but according to God's
grace.

# Charity

**PROVERBS 14:21**
Blessed is he who is kind to the needy.

**PSALM 41:1-2**
Blessed is he who has regard for the weak;
the LORD delivers him in times of trouble.
The LORD will protect him and preserve his life;
he will bless him in the land
and not surrender him to the desire of his foes.

**PROVERBS 28:27**
He who gives to the poor will lack nothing,
but he who closes his eyes to them receives
many curses.

**PROVERBS 19:17**
He who is kind to the poor lends to the Lord,
and he will reward him for what he has done.

**MATTHEW 25:40**
The King will reply, "I tell you the truth, whatever
you did for one of the least of these brothers of mine,
you did for me."

## PROVERBS 11:25

A generous man will prosper;
he who refreshes others will himself be
refreshed.

## MATTHEW 10:42

If anyone gives even a cup of cold water to one of
these little ones because he is my disciple, I tell you
the truth, he will certainly not lose his reward.

## PROVERBS 22:9

A generous man will himself be blessed,
for he shares his food with the poor.

## LUKE 14:13-14

When you give a banquet, invite the poor, the crip-
pled, the lame, the blind, and you will be blessed.
Although they cannot repay you, you will be repaid at
the resurrection of the righteous.

## 2 CORINTHIANS 9:7

Each man should give what he has decided in his
heart to give, not reluctantly or under compulsion,
for God loves a cheerful giver.

# Children

**PSALM 127:3-5**

Sons are a heritage from the LORD,
children a reward from him.
Like arrows in the hands of a warrior
are sons born in one's youth.
Blessed is the man
whose quiver is full of them.

**PROVERBS 22:6**

Train a child in the way he should go,
and when he is old he will not turn from it.

**PROVERBS 29:17**

Discipline your son, and he will give you peace;
he will bring delight to your soul.

**PROVERBS 20:11**

Even a child is known by his actions,
by whether his conduct is pure and right.

### 3 JOHN 1:4

I have no greater joy than to hear that my children
are walking in the truth.

### PSALM 139:13

For you created my inmost being;
you knit me together in my mother's womb.

### PSALM 22:10

From birth I was cast upon you;
from my mother's womb you have been
my God.

### PSALM 71:6

From birth I have relied on you;
you brought me forth from my mother's womb.
I will ever praise you.

### MATTHEW 18:4

Whoever humbles himself like this child is the great-
est in the kingdom of heaven.

## MARK 10:15

I tell you the truth, anyone who will not receive the
kingdom of God like a little child will never enter it.

## DEUTERONOMY 11:18-21

Fix these words of mine in your hearts and minds; tie
them as symbols on your hands and bind them on
your foreheads. Teach them to your children, talking
about them when you sit at home and when you
walk along the road, when you lie down and when
you get up. Write them on the doorframes of your
houses and on your gates, so that your days and the
days of your children may be many in the land that
the LORD swore to give your forefathers, as many as
the days that the heavens are above the earth.

## PSALM 139:14-16

I praise you because I am fearfully and wonderfully
    made;
    your works are wonderful,
    I know that full well.
My frame was not hidden from you
    when I was made in the secret place.
When I was woven together in the depths of the
    earth,

your eyes saw my unformed body.
All the days ordained for me
   were written in your book
   before one of them came to be.


PSALM 78:5-7
   He decreed statutes for Jacob
      and established the law in Israel,
   which he commanded our forefathers
      to teach their children,
   so the next generation would know them,
      even the children yet to be born,
      and they in turn would tell their children.
   Then they would put their trust in God
      and would not forget his deeds
      but would keep his commands.


ACTS 2:38-39
Peter replied, "Repent and be baptized, every one of
you, in the name of Jesus Christ for the forgiveness of
your sins. And you will receive the gift of the Holy
Spirit. The promise is for you and your children and
for all who are far off—for all whom the Lord our
God will call."

# Children of God

**2 CORINTHIANS 6:18**
"I will be a Father to you,
    and you will be my sons and daughters,"
    says the Lord Almighty.

**JOHN 1:12-13**
Yet to all who received him, to those who believed in
his name, he gave the right to become children of
God—children born not of natural descent, nor of
human decision or a husband's will, but born of God.

**ROMANS 8:16**
The Spirit himself testifies with our spirit that we are
God's children.

**ROMANS 8:14-15**
Those who are led by the Spirit of God are sons of
God. For you did not receive a spirit that makes you
a slave again to fear, but you received the Spirit of
sonship. And by him we cry, "Abba, Father."

**GALATIANS 4:6-7**
Because you are sons, God sent the Spirit of his Son

into our hearts, the Spirit who calls out, "Abba, Father." So you are no longer a slave, but a son; and since you are a son, God has made you also an heir.

### 1 JOHN 3:1
How great is the love the Father has lavished on us, that we should be called children of God! And that is what we are! The reason the world does not know us is that it did not know him.

### 1 JOHN 3:2
Dear friends, now we are children of God, and what we will be has not yet been made known. But we know that when he appears, we shall be like him, for we shall see him as he is.

### EPHESIANS 5:1-2
Be imitators of God, therefore, as dearly loved children and live a life of love, just as Christ loved us and gave himself up for us as a fragrant offering and sacrifice to God.

### GALATIANS 3:26, 28
You are all sons of God through faith in Christ Jesus... There is neither Jew nor Greek, slave nor free, male nor female, for you are all one in Christ Jesus.

# Children's Duties

**DEUTERONOMY 5:16**

Honor your father and your mother, as the LORD your God has commanded you, so that you may live long and that it may go well with you in the land the LORD your God is giving you.

**EPHESIANS 6:2**

"Honor your father and mother"—which is the first commandment with a promise.

**COLOSSIANS 3:20**

Children, obey your parents in everything, for this pleases the Lord.

**PROVERBS 8:32-33**

Now then, my sons, listen to me;
    blessed are those who keep my ways.
Listen to my instruction and be wise;
    do not ignore it.

**PROVERBS 23:22**

Listen to your father, who gave you life,
    and do not despise your mother when she is old.

## PROVERBS 6:20-22

My son, keep your father's commands
and do not forsake your mother's teaching.
Bind them upon your heart forever;
fasten them around your neck.
When you walk, they will guide you;
when you sleep, they will watch over you;
when you awake, they will speak to you.

## PSALM 119:9

How can a young man keep his way pure?
By living according to your word.

## PROVERBS 23:25

May your father and mother be glad;
may she who gave you birth rejoice!

## 1 TIMOTHY 5:4

If a widow has children or grandchildren, these
should learn first of all to put their religion into practice by caring for their own family and so repaying
their parents and grandparents, for this is pleasing to
God.

# Christ's Return

**HEBREWS 9:28**
So Christ was sacrificed once to take away the sins of many people; and he will appear a second time, not to bear sin, but to bring salvation to those who are waiting for him.

**JOHN 14:2-3**
In my Father's house are many rooms; if it were not so, I would have told you. I am going there to prepare a place for you. And if I go and prepare a place for you, I will come back and take you to be with me that you also may be where I am.

**ACTS 1:11**
"Men of Galilee," they said, "why do you stand here looking into the sky? This same Jesus, who has been taken from you into heaven, will come back in the same way you have seen him go into heaven."

**REVELATION 1:7**
Look, he is coming with the clouds,
and every eye will see him.

## 1 THESSALONIANS 4:16

For the Lord himself will come down from heaven, with a loud command, with the voice of the archangel and with the trumpet call of God, and the dead in Christ will rise first.

## REVELATION 22:12

Behold, I am coming soon! My reward is with me, and I will give to everyone according to what he has done.

## 2 PETER 3:10

The day of the Lord will come like a thief. The heavens will disappear with a roar; the elements will be destroyed by fire, and the earth and everything in it will be laid bare.

## LUKE 12:40

You also must be ready, because the Son of Man will come at an hour when you do not expect him.

## MATTHEW 24:14

This gospel of the kingdom will be preached in the whole world as a testimony to all nations, and then the end will come.

# Church

## 1 PETER 2:9

You are a chosen people, a royal priesthood, a holy
nation, a people belonging to God, that you may
declare the praises of him who called you out of darkness into his wonderful light.

## 1 TIMOTHY 3:15

God's household ... is the church of the living God,
the pillar and foundation of the truth.

## 1 CORINTHIANS 12:27-28

Now you are the body of Christ, and each one of you
is a part of it.

And in the church God has appointed first of all
apostles, second prophets, third teachers, then work-
ers of miracles, also those having gifts of healing,
those able to help others, those with gifts of adminis-
tration, and those speaking in different kinds of
tongues.

## 1 CORINTHIANS 12:12-13

The body is a unit, though it is made up of many parts; and though all its parts are many, they form one body. So it is with Christ. For we were all baptized by one Spirit into one body—whether Jews or Greeks, slave or free—and we were all given the one Spirit to drink.

## COLOSSIANS 1:18

He is the head of the body, the church; he is the beginning and the firstborn from among the dead, so that in everything he might have the supremacy.

## ROMANS 12:4-6

Just as each of us has one body with many members, and these members do not all have the same function, so in Christ we who are many form one body, and each member belongs to all the others. We have different gifts, according to the grace given us. If a man's gift is prophesying, let him use it in proportion to his faith.

## EPHESIANS 4:11-13

It was he who gave some to be apostles, some to be prophets, some to be evangelists, and some to be

pastors and teachers, to prepare God's people for
works of service, so that the body of Christ may be
built up until we all reach unity in the faith and in
the knowledge of the Son of God and become
mature, attaining to the whole measure of the fullness
of Christ.

HEBREWS 13:17
Obey your leaders and submit to their authority.
They keep watch over you as men who must give
an account. Obey them so that their work will be a
joy, not a burden, for that would be of no advantage
to you.

COLOSSIANS 3:16
Let the word of Christ dwell in you richly as you
teach and admonish one another with all wisdom,
and as you sing psalms, hymns and spiritual songs
with gratitude in your hearts to God.

ACTS 2:42-47
They devoted themselves to the apostles' teaching and
to the fellowship, to the breaking of bread and to
prayer.

Everyone was filled with awe, and many wonders and miraculous signs were done by the apostles. All the believers were together and had everything in common. Selling their possessions and goods, they gave to anyone as he had need. Every day they continued to meet together in the temple courts. They broke bread in their homes and ate together with glad and sincere hearts, praising God and enjoying the favor of all the people. And the Lord added to their number daily those who were being saved.

MATTHEW 16:17-18
Jesus replied, "Blessed are you, Simon son of Jonah, for this was not revealed to you by man, but by my Father in heaven. And I tell you that you are Peter, and on this rock I will build my church, and the gates of Hades will not overcome it."

# Comfort

**2 CORINTHIANS 1:3-4**
Praise be to the God and Father of our LORD Jesus
Christ, the Father of compassion and the God of all
comfort, who comforts us in all our troubles, so that
we can comfort those in any trouble with the comfort
we ourselves have received from God.

**ISAIAH 66:13**
As a mother comforts her child,
so will I comfort you;
and you will be comforted over Jerusalem.

**PSALM 34:18**
The LORD is close to the brokenhearted
and saves those who are crushed in spirit.

**REVELATION 7:17**
For the Lamb at the center of the throne will be
their shepherd;
he will lead them to springs of living water.
And God will wipe away every tear from their
eyes.

**DEUTERONOMY 33:12b**
Let the beloved of the Lord rest secure in him, for he shields him all day long and the one the Lord loves rests between his shoulders.

**ISAIAH 57:18-19**
"I have seen his ways, but I will heal him;
    I will guide him and restore comfort to him,
creating praise on the lips of the mourners in
        Israel.
Peace, peace, to those far and near,"
says the LORD. "And I will heal them."

**JEREMIAH 31:13**
Then maidens will dance and be glad,
        young men and old as well.
I will turn their mourning into gladness;
    I will give them comfort and joy instead
        of sorrow.

# Commitment

**PSALM 37:5**

Commit your way to the LORD;
    trust in him and he will do this.

**PROVERBS 16:3**

Commit to the LORD whatever you do,
    and your plans will succeed.

**1 KINGS 8:61**

Your hearts must be fully committed to the LORD
our God, to live by his decrees and obey his commands, as at this time.

**2 CHRONICLES 16:9**

For the eyes of the LORD range throughout the earth
to strengthen those whose hearts are fully committed
to him.

**PSALM 103:17-18**

From everlasting to everlasting
    the LORD's love is with those who fear him,

and his righteousness with their children's
children—
with those who keep his covenant
and remember to obey his precepts.

PSALM 132:12
If your sons keep my covenant
and the statutes I teach them,
then their sons will sit
on your throne for ever and ever.

NUMBERS 30:2
When a man makes a vow to the LORD or takes an
oath to obligate himself by a pledge, he must not
break his word but must do everything he said.

DEUTERONOMY 23:21
If you make a vow to the LORD your God, do not be
slow to pay it, for the LORD your God will certainly
demand it of you and you will be guilty of sin.

ECCLESIASTES 5:4
When you make a vow to God, do not delay in ful-
filling it. He has no pleasure in fools; fulfill your vow.

# Compassion

**NEHEMIAH 9:17**
You are a forgiving God, gracious and compassionate,
slow to anger and abounding in love.

**PSALM 145:9**
The LORD is good to all;
  he has compassion on all he has made.

**ISAIAH 30:18**
Yet the LORD longs to be gracious to you;
  he rises to show you compassion.
For the LORD is a God of justice.
  Blessed are all who wait for him!

**PSALM 103:13**
As a father has compassion on his children,
  so the LORD has compassion on those who fear
    him.

**HOSEA 2:19**
I will betroth you to me forever;

I will betroth you in righteousness and justice,
in love and compassion.

ISAIAH 54:10
"Though the mountains be shaken
and the hills be removed,
yet my unfailing love for you will not be shaken
nor my covenant of peace be removed,"
says the LORD, who has compassion on you.

PSALM 119:156
Your compassion is great, O LORD;
preserve my life according to your laws.

LAMENTATIONS 3:22-23
Because of the LORD's great love we are not
consumed,
for his compassions never fail.
They are new every morning;
great is your faithfulness.

2 CORINTHIANS 1:3
Praise be to the God and Father of our Lord Jesus
Christ, the Father of compassion and the God of all
comfort.

# Confidence

**PROVERBS 3:26**

For the LORD will be your confidence
and will keep your foot from being snared.

**HEBREWS 13:6**

We say with confidence,
"The Lord is my helper; I will not be afraid.
What can man do to me?"

**PSALM 27:3**

Though an army besiege me,
my heart will not fear;
though war break out against me,
even then will I be confident.

**PSALM 23:4**

Even though I walk
through the valley of the shadow of death,
I will fear no evil,
for you are with me;
your rod and your staff,
they comfort me.

## 1 JOHN 4:16-17

We know and rely on the love God has for us.

God is love. Whoever lives in love lives in God, and God in him. In this way, love is made complete among us so that we will have confidence on the day of judgment, because in this world we are like him.

## ISAIAH 32:17

The fruit of righteousness will be peace;
the effect of righteousness will be quietness and confidence forever.

## 1 JOHN 2:28

Now, dear children, continue in him, so that when he appears we may be confident and unashamed before him at his coming.

## HEBREWS 4:16

Let us then approach the throne of grace with confidence, so that we may receive mercy and find grace to help us in our time of need.

## 1 JOHN 5:14

This is the confidence we have in approaching God: that if we ask anything according to his will, he hears us.

# Consolation

**PSALM 147:3**

He heals the brokenhearted
and binds up their wounds.

**PSALM 34:18**

The LORD is close to the brokenhearted
and saves those who are crushed in spirit.

**REVELATION 14:13**

Then I heard a voice from heaven say, "Write: Blessed
are the dead who die in the Lord from now on."

"Yes," says the Spirit, "they will rest from their
labor, for their deeds will follow them."

**PSALM 116:15**

Precious in the sight of the LORD
is the death of his saints.

**PHILIPPIANS 1:21**

For to me, to live is Christ and to die is gain.

ROMANS 14:8

If we live, we live to the Lord; and if we die, we die to the Lord. So, whether we live or die, we belong to the Lord.

2 CORINTHIANS 5:8

We are confident, I say, and would prefer to be away from the body and at home with the Lord.

2 CORINTHIANS 1:3-4

Praise be to the God and Father of our Lord Jesus Christ, the Father of compassion and the God of all comfort, who comforts us in all our troubles, so that we can comfort those in any trouble with the comfort we ourselves have received from God.

# Contentment

**PHILIPPIANS 4:11-12**

I am not saying this because I am in need, for I have learned to be content whatever the circumstances. I know what it is to be in need, and I know what it is to have plenty. I have learned the secret of being content in any and every situation, whether well fed or hungry, whether living in plenty or in want.

**PROVERBS 19:23**

The fear of the LORD leads to life:
    Then one rests content, untouched by trouble.

**1 TIMOTHY 6:6**

Godliness with contentment is great gain.

**HEBREWS 13:5**

Keep your lives free from the love of money and be content with what you have, because God has said,
    "Never will I leave you;
    never will I forsake you."

**JOB 1:21**

Naked I came from my mother's womb,
    and naked I will depart.

The LORD gave and the LORD has taken away;
may the name of the LORD be praised.

## 1 TIMOTHY 6:8

If we have food and clothing, we will be content with
that.

## PSALM 16:2

I said to the LORD, "You are my LORD;
apart from you I have no good thing."

## PROVERBS 15:15

The cheerful heart has a continual feast.

## LUKE 3:11-14

John answered, "The man with two tunics should
share with him who has none, and the one who has
food should do the same." Tax collectors also came to
be baptized. "Teacher," they asked, "what should we
do?" "Don't collect any more than you are required
to," he told them. Then some soldiers asked him,
"And what should we do?" He replied, "Don't extort
money and don't accuse people falsely—be content
with your pay."

# Courage

**PSALM 31:24**

Be strong and take heart,
all you who hope in the LORD.

**PSALM 27:14**

Wait for the LORD;
be strong and take heart
and wait for the LORD.

**ISAIAH 43:2-3**

When you pass through the waters,
I will be with you;
and when you pass through the rivers,
they will not sweep over you.
When you walk through the fire,
you will not be burned;
the flames will not set you ablaze.
For I am the LORD, your God,
the Holy One of Israel, your Savior.

**DEUTERONOMY 7:21**

The LORD your God, who is among you, is a great
and awesome God.

PSALM 28:7
> The LORD is my strength and my shield;
>> my heart trusts in him, and I am helped.
> My heart leaps for joy
> and I will give thanks to him in song.

ISAIAH 41:10
> I will strengthen you and help you;
>> I will uphold you with my righteous right hand.

PSALM 18:32
> It is God who arms me with strength
>> and makes my way perfect.

ISAIAH 40:29
> He gives strength to the weary
>> and increases the power of the weak.

PSALM 18:29
> With your help I can advance against a troop;
>> with my God I can scale a wall.

ISAIAH 50:7
> Because the Sovereign LORD helps me,
>> I will not be disgraced.
> Therefore have I set my face like flint,
>> and I know I will not be put to shame.

# Daily Walk

## DEUTERONOMY 5:33

Walk in all the way that the LORD your God has
commanded you, so that you may live and prosper
and prolong your days in the land that you will possess.

## PROVERBS 4:25-26

Let your eyes look straight ahead,
    fix your gaze directly before you.
Make level paths for your feet
    and take only ways that are firm.

## GALATIANS 5:25

Since we live by the Spirit, let us keep in step with the
Spirit.

## COLOSSIANS 3:23

Whatever you do, work at it with all your heart, as
working for the Lord, not for men.

## 1 THESSALONIANS 4:1

Finally, brothers, we instructed you how to live in
order to please God, as in fact you are living. Now we

ask you and urge you in the Lord Jesus to do this
more and more.

## 1 TIMOTHY 6:11-12

Flee from all this, and pursue righteousness, godliness,
faith, love, endurance and gentleness. Fight the good
fight of the faith. Take hold of the eternal life to
which you were called when you made your good
confession in the presence of many witnesses.

## COLOSSIANS 1:10

We pray this in order that you may live a life worthy
of the Lord and may please him in every way: bearing
fruit in every good work, growing in the knowledge
of God.

## EPHESIANS 5:15

Be very careful, then, how you live—not as unwise
but as wise.

## PROVERBS 14:15

A simple man believes anything,
    but a prudent man gives thought to his steps.

# Decisions

**JEREMIAH 6:16**
This is what the LORD says:
"Stand at the crossroads and look;
    ask for the ancient paths,
ask where the good way is, and walk in it,
    and you will find rest for your souls."

**JAMES 1:5**
If any of you lacks wisdom, he should ask God, who gives generously to all without finding fault, and it will be given to him.

**JEREMIAH 33:3**
Call to me and I will answer you and tell you great and unsearchable things you do not know.

**JOHN 14:16, 17**
I will ask the Father, and he will give you another Counselor to be with you forever—the Spirit of truth. The world cannot accept him, because it neither sees him nor knows him. But you know him, for he lives with you and will be in you.

HAGGAI 1:5
Now this is what the LORD Almighty says: "Give careful thought to your ways."

PROVERBS 3:5-6
Trust in the LORD with all your heart
     and lean not on your own understanding;
in all your ways acknowledge him,
     and he will make your paths straight.

PROVERBS 16:9
In his heart a man plans his course,
     but the LORD determines his steps.

PSALM 37:5
Commit your way to the LORD;
     trust in him.

PSALM 37:23
If the LORD delights in a man's way,
     he makes his steps firm.

PSALM 37:4
Delight yourself in the LORD
     and he will give you the desires of your heart.

# Deliverance

**2 SAMUEL 22:1**
David sang to the LORD the words of this song when
the Lord delivered him from the hand of all his enemies and from the hand of Saul.

**2 SAMUEL 22:2**
He said:
"The LORD is my rock, my fortress and my deliverer."

**PSALM 34:17**
The righteous cry out, and the LORD hears them;
    he delivers them from all their troubles.

**PSALM 107:6**
They cried out to the LORD in their trouble,
    and he delivered them from their distress.

**2 PETER 2:9**
The Lord knows how to rescue godly men from trials
and to hold the unrighteous for the day of judgment,
while continuing their punishment.

PSALM 34:7

The angel of the LORD encamps around those
who fear him,
and he delivers them.

PSALM 32:7

You are my hiding place;
you will protect me from trouble
and surround me with songs of deliverance.

PSALM 116:8

For you, O LORD, have delivered my soul from
death,
my eyes from tears,
my feet from stumbling.

PSALM 91:14-15

"Because he loves me," says the LORD, "I will
rescue him;
I will protect him, for he acknowledges my
name.
He will call upon me, and I will answer him;
I will be with him in trouble,
I will deliver him and honor him."

# Determination

**ISAIAH 50:7**

> Because the Sovereign LORD helps me,
>    I will not be disgraced.
> Therefore have I set my face like flint,
>    and I know I will not be put to shame.

**1 CORINTHIANS 15:58**

My dear brothers, stand firm. Let nothing move you. Always give yourselves fully to the work of the Lord, because you know that your labor in the Lord is not in vain.

**REVELATION 3:11**

I am coming soon. Hold on to what you have, so that no one will take your crown.

**GALATIANS 6:9**

Let us not become weary in doing good, for at the proper time we will reap a harvest if we do not give up.

## 1 PETER 5:8-9

Be self-controlled and alert. Your enemy the devil
prowls around like a roaring lion looking for someone
to devour. Resist him, standing firm in the faith,
because you know that your brothers throughout the
world are undergoing the same kind of sufferings.

## DEUTERONOMY 4:9

Only be careful, and watch yourselves closely so that
you do not forget the things your eyes have seen or let
them slip from your heart as long as you live. Teach
them to your children and to their children after
them.

## PSALM 17:3

Though you probe my heart and examine me at
night,

though you test me, you will find nothing;
I have resolved that my mouth will not sin.

## PSALM 119:11

I have hidden your word in my heart
that I might not sin against you.

# Devotion

### JOB 11:13, 15, 18

If you devote your heart to him
and stretch out your hands to him ...
then you will lift up your face without shame;
you will stand firm and without fear ...
You will be secure, because there is hope;
you will look about you and take your rest in
safety.

### ACTS 2:41-47

Those who accepted his message were baptized, and
about three thousand were added to their number
that day.

They devoted themselves to the apostles' teaching
and to the fellowship, to the breaking of bread and to
prayer. Everyone was filled with awe, and many wonders and miraculous signs were done by the apostles.
All the believers were together and had everything in
common. Selling their possessions and goods, they
gave to anyone as he had need. Every day they continued to meet together in the temple courts. They
broke bread in their homes and ate together with glad

and sincere hearts, praising God and enjoying the
favor of all the people. And the Lord added to their
number daily those who were being saved.

PSALM 141:8

My eyes are fixed on you, O Sovereign LORD;
    in you I take refuge.

DEUTERONOMY 6:5

Love the LORD your God with all your heart and
with all your soul and with all your strength.

PSALM 86:2

Guard my life, for I am devoted to you.
    You are my God; save your servant
    who trusts in you.

2 CHRONICLES 16:9

For the eyes of the LORD range throughout the earth
to strengthen those whose hearts are fully committed
to him.

# Discernment

**JOHN 16:13**
When he, the Spirit of truth, comes, he will guide
you into all truth. He will not speak on his own; he
will speak only what he hears, and he will tell you
what is yet to come.

**2 TIMOTHY 2:7**
Reflect on what I am saying, for the Lord will give
you insight into all this.

**JOHN 16:15**
All that belongs to the Father is mine. That is why I
said the Spirit will take from what is mine and make
it known to you.

**1 JOHN 4:6**
We are from God, and whoever knows God listens to
us; but whoever is not from God does not listen to
us. This is how we recognize the Spirit of truth and
the spirit of falsehood.

## 1 JOHN 4:1

Test the spirits to see whether they are from God, because many false prophets have gone out into the world.

## 1 THESSALONIANS 5:21-22

Test everything. Hold on to the good. Avoid every kind of evil.

## 1 JOHN 2:3

We know that we have come to know him if we obey his commands.

## 1 CORINTHIANS 2:14-16

The man without the Spirit does not accept the things that come from the Spirit of God, for they are foolishness to him, and he cannot understand them, because they are spiritually discerned. The spiritual man makes judgments about all things, but he himself is not subject to any man's judgment:

"For who has known the mind of the Lord
    that he may instruct him?"

But we have the mind of Christ.

# Discipleship

**JOHN 12:26**

Whoever serves me must follow me; and where I am, my servant also will be. My Father will honor the one who serves me.

**JOHN 10:27**

My sheep listen to my voice; I know them, and they follow me.

**JOHN 8:12**

When Jesus spoke again to the people, he said, "I am the light of the world. Whoever follows me will never walk in darkness, but will have the light of life."

**JOB 36:11**

If they obey and serve him,
    they will spend the rest of their days in
        prosperity
and their years in contentment.

## JOHN 14:21

Whoever has my commands and obeys them, he is the one who loves me. He who loves me will be loved by my Father, and I too will love him and show myself to him.

## JOHN 8:31

To the Jews who had believed him, Jesus said, "If you hold to my teaching, you are really my disciples."

## JOHN 15:8

This is to my Father's glory, that you bear much fruit, showing yourselves to be my disciples.

## JOHN 13:35

By this all men will know that you are my disciples, if you love one another.

## 2 TIMOTHY 4:1-2

In the presence of God and of Christ Jesus, who will judge the living and the dead, and in view of his appearing and his kingdom, I give you this charge: Preach the Word; be prepared in season and out of season; correct, rebuke and encourage—with great patience and careful instruction.

# Elderly

**TITUS 2:2-4**

Teach the older men to be temperate, worthy of respect, self-controlled, and sound in faith, in love and in endurance.

Likewise, teach the older women to be reverent in the way they live, not to be slanderers or addicted to much wine, but to teach what is good. Then they can train the younger women to love their husbands and children.

**1 CORINTHIANS 13:11**

When I was a child, I talked like a child, I thought like a child, I reasoned like a child. When I became a man, I put childish ways behind me.

**PROVERBS 3:1-2**

My son, do not forget my teaching,
    but keep my commands in your heart,
for they will prolong your life many years
    and bring you prosperity.

**PROVERBS 9:11**

For through me your days will be many,
    and years will be added to your life.

**PSALM 92:12-14**

The righteous will flourish like a palm tree,
they will grow like a cedar of Lebanon;
planted in the house of the LORD,
they will flourish in the courts of our God.
They will still bear fruit in old age,
they will stay fresh and green.

**PROVERBS 16:31**

Gray hair is a crown of splendor;
it is attained by a righteous life.

**PSALM 71:17-18**

Since my youth, O God, you have taught me,
and to this day I declare your marvelous deeds.
Even when I am old and gray,
do not forsake me, O God,
till I declare your power to the next generation,
your might to all who are to come.

**PSALM 37:25**

I was young and now I am old,
yet I have never seen the righteous forsaken
or their children begging bread.

**ISAIAH 46:4**

Even to your old age and gray hairs I am he,
I am he who will sustain you.
I have made you and I will carry you;
I will sustain you and I will rescue you.

# Encouragement

**2 THESSALONIANS 2:16-17**
May our Lord Jesus Christ himself and God our
Father, who loved us and by his grace gave us eternal
encouragement and good hope, encourage your
hearts and strengthen you in every good deed and
word.

**PSALM 10:17**
You hear, O LORD, the desire of the afflicted;
   you encourage them, and you listen to their cry.

**LAMENTATIONS 3:25-26**
The LORD is good to those whose hope is in him,
   to the one who seeks him;
it is good to wait quietly
   for the salvation of the LORD.

**JEREMIAH 29:11**
"For I know the plans I have for you," declares the
LORD, "plans to prosper you and not to harm you,
plans to give you hope and a future."

## 2 CORINTHIANS 4:16

Though outwardly we are wasting away, yet inwardly
we are being renewed day by day.

## LAMENTATIONS 3:21-23

This I call to mind
and therefore I have hope:
Because of the LORD's great love we are not
consumed,
for his compassions never fail.
They are new every morning;
great is your faithfulness.

## PSALM 68:19

Praise be to the Lord, to God our Savior,
who daily bears our burdens.

## PSALM 55:22

Cast your cares on the LORD
and he will sustain you;
he will never let the righteous fall.

## 1 THESSALONIANS 5:11

Encourage one another and build each other up, just
as in fact you are doing.

# Eternal Life

**1 JOHN 2:17**
The world and its desires pass away, but the man who does the will of God lives forever.

**ROMANS 6:23**
For the wages of sin is death, but the gift of God is eternal life in Christ Jesus our Lord.

**JOHN 3:16**
For God so loved the world that he gave his one and only Son, that whoever believes in him shall not perish but have eternal life.

**1 JOHN 5:11-12**
This is the testimony: God has given us eternal life, and this life is in his Son. He who has the Son has life; he who does not have the Son of God does not have life.

**JOHN 11:25-26**
Jesus said to her, "I am the resurrection and the life. He who believes in me will live, even though he dies;

and whoever lives and believes in me will never die.
Do you believe this?"

JOHN 3:36
Whoever believes in the Son has eternal life.

TITUS 3:7
Having been justified by his grace, we might become
heirs having the hope of eternal life.

JOHN 10:27-29
My sheep listen to my voice; I know them, and they
follow me. I give them eternal life, and they shall
never perish; no one can snatch them out of my
hand. My Father, who has given them to me, is
greater than all; no one can snatch them out of my
Father's hand.

JOHN 17:3
Now this is eternal life: that they may know you,
the only true God, and Jesus Christ, whom you
have sent.

# Expectancy

### PSALM 37:7

Be still before the LORD and wait patiently for him;
do not fret when men succeed in their ways,
when they carry out their wicked schemes.

### HOSEA 6:3

Let us acknowledge the LORD;
let us press on to acknowledge him.
As surely as the sun rises,
he will appear;
he will come to us like the winter rains,
like the spring rains that water the earth.

### PSALM 27:14

Wait for the LORD;
be strong and take heart
and wait for the LORD.

### ISAIAH 26:8

Yes, LORD, walking in the way of your laws,
we wait for you;
your name and renown
are the desire of our hearts.

## MICAH 7:7

As for me, I watch in hope for the LORD,
  I wait for God my Savior;
  my God will hear me.

## PSALM 130:5

I wait for the LORD, my soul waits,
  and in his word I put my hope.

## PSALM 40:1-2

I waited patiently for the LORD;
  he turned to me and heard my cry.
He lifted me out of the slimy pit,
out of the mud and mire;
  he set my feet on a rock
  and gave me a firm place to stand.

## ISAIAH 25:9

In that day they will say,

"Surely this is our God;
  we trusted in him, and he saved us.
This is the LORD, we trusted in him;
  let us rejoice and be glad in his salvation."

# Faith

### HEBREWS 11:1
Now faith is being sure of what we hope for and
certain of what we do not see.

### 1 PETER 1:21
Through him you believe in God, who raised him
from the dead and glorified him, and so your faith
and hope are in God.

### 1 PETER 1:8
Though you have not seen him, you love him; and even
though you do not see him now, you believe in him
and are filled with an inexpressible and glorious joy.

### 1 TIMOTHY 4:9-10
This is a trustworthy saying that deserves full acceptance (and for this we labor and strive), that we have
put our hope in the living God, who is the Savior of
all men, and especially of those who believe.

### PSALM 33:22
May your unfailing love rest upon us, O LORD,
even as we put our hope in you.

ROMANS 4:3
What does the Scripture say? "Abraham believed
God, and it was credited to him as righteousness."

ROMANS 5:1
Since we have been justified through faith, we have
peace with God through our Lord Jesus Christ.

JOHN 14:12
I tell you the truth, anyone who has faith in me will
do what I have been doing. He will do even greater
things than these, because I am going to the Father.

MATTHEW 17:20
I tell you the truth, if you have faith as small as a
mustard seed, you can say to this mountain, "Move
from here to there" and it will move. Nothing will be
impossible for you.

ISAIAH 40:31
But those who hope in the LORD
    will renew their strength.
They will soar on wings like eagles;
    they will run and not grow weary,
    they will walk and not be faint.

# Faithfulness

**PROVERBS 3:3-4**

Let love and faithfulness never leave you;
bind them around your neck,
write them on the tablet of your heart.
Then you will win favor and a good name
in the sight of God and man.

**PSALM 31:23**

Love the LORD, all his saints!
The LORD preserves the faithful,
but the proud he pays back in full.

**2 SAMUEL 22:26**

To the faithful you show yourself faithful,
to the blameless you show yourself blameless.

**PSALM 37:28**

For the LORD loves the just
and will not forsake his faithful ones.

PROVERBS 2:7-8

   He holds victory in store for the upright,
      he is a shield to those whose walk is blameless,
   for he guards the course of the just
      and protects the way of his faithful ones.

ISAIAH 26:3

   You will keep in perfect peace
      him whose mind is steadfast,
      because he trusts in you.

REVELATION 2:10

Be faithful, even to the point of death, and I will give
you the crown of life.

REVELATION 13:10

   If anyone is to go into captivity,
      into captivity he will go.
   If anyone is to be killed
      with the sword, with the sword he will be
         killed.

This calls for patient endurance and faithfulness on
the part of the saints.

# Faithfulness of God

**1 CORINTHIANS 1:9**
God, who has called you into fellowship with his Son
Jesus Christ our Lord, is faithful.

**PSALM 100:5**
For the LORD is good and his love endures forever;
his faithfulness continues through all
generations.

**ISAIAH 54:10**
"Though the mountains be shaken
and the hills be removed,
yet my unfailing love for you will not be shaken
nor my covenant of peace be removed,"
says the LORD, who has compassion on you.

**LAMENTATIONS 3:22-23**
Because of the LORD's great love we are not
consumed,
for his compassions never fail.
They are new every morning;
great is your faithfulness.

## PSALM 111:7-8

> The works of his hands are faithful and just;
> > all his precepts are trustworthy.
> They are steadfast for ever and ever,
> > done in faithfulness and uprightness.

## DEUTERONOMY 7:9

Know therefore that the LORD your God is God; he is the faithful God, keeping his covenant of love to a thousand generations of those who love him and keep his commands.

## PSALM 18:25

> To the faithful you show yourself faithful,
> > to the blameless you show yourself blameless.

## 1 JOHN 1:9

If we confess our sins, he is faithful and just and will forgive us our sins and purify us from all unrighteousness.

## PSALM 108:4

> For great is your love, higher than the heavens;
> > your faithfulness reaches to the skies.

## 2 THESSALONIANS 3:3

The Lord is faithful, and he will strengthen and protect you from the evil one.

# Family

**JOSHUA 24:15**

Choose for yourselves this day whom you will serve ...
But as for me and my household, we will serve the
LORD.

**GENESIS 18:19**

For I have chosen him, so that he will direct his children and his household after him to keep the way of
the LORD by doing what is right and just, so that the
LORD will bring about for Abraham what he has
promised him.

**PSALM 78:5-7**

He decreed statutes for Jacob
    and established the law in Israel,
which he commanded our forefathers
    to teach their children,
so the next generation would know them,
    even the children yet to be born,
and they in turn would tell their children.
    Then they would put their trust in God
and would not forget his deeds
    but would keep his commands.

## 1 TIMOTHY 3:2-4

Now the overseer must be above reproach, the husband of but one wife, temperate, self-controlled, respectable, hospitable, able to teach, not given to drunkenness, not violent but gentle, not quarrelsome, not a lover of money. He must manage his own family well and see that his children obey him with proper respect.

## TITUS 2:3-5

Likewise, teach the older women to be reverent in the way they live, not to be slanderers or addicted to much wine, but to teach what is good. Then they can train the younger women to love their husbands and children, to be self-controlled and pure, to be busy at home, to be kind, and to be subject to their husbands, so that no one will malign the word of God.

## PROVERBS 31:15

She gets up while it is still dark;
 she provides food for her family
 and portions for her servant girls.

## ISAIAH 32:18

My people will live in peaceful dwelling places,
 in secure homes,
 in undisturbed places of rest.

# Fellowship

### 1 JOHN 4:12
No one has ever seen God; but if we love one another, God lives in us and his love is made complete in us.

### JAMES 2:8
If you really keep the royal law found in Scripture, "Love your neighbor as yourself," you are doing right.

### MATTHEW 5:44-45
I tell you: Love your enemies and pray for those who persecute you, that you may be sons of your Father in heaven.

### 1 PETER 4:8
Above all, love each other deeply, because love covers over a multitude of sins.

### LUKE 6:31
Do to others as you would have them do to you.

**PHILIPPIANS 2:3-4**
In humility consider others better than yourselves.
Each of you should look not only to your own inter-
ests, but also to the interests of others.

**COLOSSIANS 3:12**
As God's chosen people, holy and dearly loved, clothe
yourselves with compassion, kindness, humility, gentleness and patience.

**ROMANS 14:19**
Let us therefore make every effort to do what leads to
peace and to mutual edification.

**EPHESIANS 4:29**
Do not let any unwholesome talk come out of your
mouths, but only what is helpful for building others
up according to their needs, that it may benefit those
who listen.

**MATTHEW 18:20**
For where two or three come together in my name,
there am I with them.

# Finances

## LUKE 12:15

He said to them, "Watch out! Be on your guard against all kinds of greed; a man's life does not consist in the abundance of his possessions."

## HEBREWS 13:5

Keep your lives free from the love of money and be content with what you have, because God has said,

"Never will I leave you;
   never will I forsake you."

## LUKE 16:10

Whoever can be trusted with very little can also be trusted with much, and whoever is dishonest with very little will also be dishonest with much.

## PROVERBS 3:9-10

Honor the LORD with your wealth,
    with the firstfruits of all your crops;
then your barns will be filled to overflowing,
    and your vats will brim over with new wine.

## MALACHI 3:10

"Bring the whole tithe into the storehouse, that there
may be food in my house. Test me in this," says the
LORD Almighty, "and see if I will not throw open the
floodgates of heaven and pour out so much blessing
that you will not have room enough for it."

## 2 CORINTHIANS 9:7

Each man should give what he has decided in his
heart to give, not reluctantly or under compulsion,
for God loves a cheerful giver.

## PROVERBS 28:27

He who gives to the poor will lack nothing,
   but he who closes his eyes to them receives
      many curses.

## LUKE 6:38

Give, and it will be given to you. A good measure,
pressed down, shaken together and running over, will
be poured into your lap. For with the measure you
use, it will be measured to you.

## ROMANS 13:8

Let no debt remain outstanding, except the continuing debt to love one another, for he who loves his fel-
lowman has fulfilled the law.

## PROVERBS 13:22

A good man leaves an inheritance for his children's
      children,
   but a sinner's wealth is stored up for the
      righteous.

## MATTHEW 6:2-4

So when you give to the needy, do not announce it
with trumpets, as the hypocrites do in the synagogues
and on the streets, to be honored by men. I tell you
the truth, they have received their reward in full. But
when you give to the needy, do not let your left hand
know what your right hand is doing, so that your giving may be in secret. Then your Father, who sees
what is done in secret, will reward you.

## DEUTERONOMY 15:7-8

If there is a poor man among your brothers in any of
the towns of the land that the LORD your God is
giving you, do not be hardhearted or tightfisted
toward your poor brother. Rather be openhanded and
freely lend him whatever he needs.

## DEUTERONOMY 15:10

Give generously to him and do so without a grudging
heart; then because of this the Lord your God will
bless you in all your work and in everything you put
your hand to.

# Forgiveness

**EPHESIANS 4:32**
Be kind and compassionate to one another, forgiving
each other, just as in Christ God forgave you.

**COLOSSIANS 3:13**
Bear with each other and forgive whatever grievances
you may have against one another. Forgive as the
Lord forgave you.

**MATTHEW 6:14**
For if you forgive men when they sin against you,
your heavenly Father will also forgive you.

**2 CORINTHIANS 2:5-7**
If anyone has caused grief, he has not so much grieved me as he has grieved all of you, to some extent—
not to put it too severely. The punishment inflicted
on him by the majority is sufficient for him. Now
instead, you ought to forgive and comfort him, so
that he will not be overwhelmed by excessive sorrow.

## 2 CORINTHIANS 2:10

If you forgive anyone, I also forgive him. And what I have forgiven—if there was anything to forgive—I have forgiven in the sight of Christ for your sake.

## LUKE 6:37

Forgive, and you will be forgiven.

## MARK 11:25

When you stand praying, if you hold anything against anyone, forgive him, so that your Father in heaven may forgive you your sins.

## PROVERBS 17:9

He who covers over an offense promotes love,
but whoever repeats the matter separates close
friends.

## PROVERBS 10:12

Love covers over all wrongs.

## MATTHEW 18:21-22

Then Peter came to Jesus and asked, "Lord, how many times shall I forgive my brother when he sins against me? Up to seven times?" Jesus answered, "I tell you, not seven times, but seventy-seven times.

# Forgiveness of God

**ACTS 2:38**
Peter replied, "Repent and be baptized, every one of you, in the name of Jesus Christ for the forgiveness of your sins. And you will receive the gift of the Holy Spirit."

**ROMANS 8:1-2**
There is now no condemnation for those who are in Christ Jesus, because through Christ Jesus the law of the Spirit of life set me free from the law of sin and death.

**EPHESIANS 1:7**
In him we have redemption through his blood, the forgiveness of sins, in accordance with the riches of God's grace

**COLOSSIANS 2:13-14**
When you were dead in your sins and in the uncircumcision of your sinful nature, God made you alive with Christ. He forgave us all our sins, having

canceled the written code, with its regulations, that was against us and that stood opposed to us; he took it away, nailing it to the cross.

**NEHEMIAH 9:17**
You are a forgiving God, gracious and compassionate, slow to anger and abounding in love.

**PSALM 86:5**
You are forgiving and good, O Lord,
    abounding in love to all who call to you.

**1 JOHN 1:9**
If we confess our sins, he is faithful and just and will forgive us our sins and purify us from all unrighteousness.

**ISAIAH 1:18**
"Come now, let us reason together,"
    says the LORD.
"Though your sins are like scarlet,
    they shall be as white as snow;
though they are red as crimson,
    they shall be like wool."

# Freedom

### ISAIAH 61:1

The Spirit of the Sovereign LORD is on me,
    because the LORD has anointed me
    to preach good news to the poor.
He has sent me to bind up the brokenhearted,
    to proclaim freedom for the captives
    and release from darkness for the prisoners.

### JOHN 8:32

You will know the truth, and the truth will set
you free.

### MALACHI 4:2

For you who revere my name, the sun of righteousness will rise with healing in its wings. And you will go out and leap like calves released from the stall.

### JOHN 8:36

If the Son sets you free, you will be free indeed.

### 2 CORINTHIANS 3:17

Now the Lord is the Spirit, and where the Spirit of
the Lord is, there is freedom.

## ROMANS 8:2
Through Christ Jesus the law of the Spirit of life set me free from the law of sin and death.

## ROMANS 6:22
Now that you have been set free from sin and have become slaves to God, the benefit you reap leads to holiness, and the result is eternal life.

## GALATIANS 5:1
It is for freedom that Christ has set us free. Stand firm, then, and do not let yourselves be burdened again by a yoke of slavery.

## ROMANS 7:6
Now, by dying to what once bound us, we have been released from the law so that we serve in the new way of the Spirit, and not in the old way of the written code.

## ROMANS 6:7
Anyone who has died has been freed from sin.

## ROMANS 8:21
The creation itself will be liberated from its bondage to decay and brought into the glorious freedom of the children of God.

# Fresh Start

**PSALM 32:5**

I acknowledged my sin to you
 and did not cover up my iniquity.
I said, "I will confess
 my transgressions to the LORD"—
and you forgave
 the guilt of my sin.

**PSALM 103:12**

As far as the east is from the west,
 so far has he removed our transgressions from us.

**LAMENTATIONS 3:22-23**

Because of the LORD's great love we are not
 consumed,
 for his compassions never fail.
They are new every morning;
 great is your faithfulness.

**PSALM 32:1-2**

Blessed is he
 whose transgressions are forgiven,
 whose sins are covered.

Blessed is the man
whose sin the LORD does not count against him
and in whose spirit is no deceit.

ISAIAH 43:18-19
Forget the former things;
do not dwell on the past.
See, I am doing a new thing!
Now it springs up; do you not perceive it?
I am making a way in the desert
and streams in the wasteland.

EZEKIEL 36:26
I will give you a new heart and put a new spirit in you; I will remove from you your heart of stone and give you a heart of flesh.

1 PETER 1:23
For you have been born again, not of perishable seed, but of imperishable, through the living and enduring word of God.

1 PETER 1:3
Praise be to the God and Father of our Lord Jesus Christ! In his great mercy he has given us new birth into a living hope through the resurrection of Jesus Christ from the dead.

# Friendship

**PROVERBS 17:17**

A friend loves at all times,
and a brother is born for adversity.

**ROMANS 12:10**

Be devoted to one another in brotherly love. Honor
one another above yourselves.

**JOHN 15:13**

Greater love has no one than this, that he lay down
his life for his friends.

**ECCLESIASTES 4:9-10**

Two are better than one,
because they have a good return for their work:
If one falls down,
his friend can help him up.
But pity the man who falls
and has no one to help him up!

**PROVERBS 18:24**

A man of many companions may come to ruin,
but there is a friend who sticks closer than a
brother.

**PROVERBS 13:20**

He who walks with the wise grows wise,
but a companion of fools suffers harm.

**PROVERBS 27:17**

As iron sharpens iron,
so one man sharpens another.

**PROVERBS 27:6**

Wounds from a friend can be trusted,
but an enemy multiplies kisses.

**PSALM 133:1**

How good and pleasant it is
when brothers live together in unity!

# Friendship of God

**REVELATION 3:20**
Here I am! I stand at the door and knock. If anyone hears my voice and opens the door, I will come in and eat with him, and he with me.

**JOHN 14:23**
Jesus replied, "If anyone loves me, he will obey my teaching. My Father will love him, and we will come to him and make our home with him."

**JAMES 2:23**
The scripture was fulfilled that says, "Abraham believed God, and it was credited to him as righteousness," and he was called God's friend.

**JOHN 15:15**
I no longer call you servants, because a servant does not know his master's business. Instead, I have called you friends, for everything that I learned from my Father I have made known to you.

## 1 CORINTHIANS 1:9

God, who has called you into fellowship with his Son
Jesus Christ our Lord, is faithful.

## 1 JOHN 1:3

We proclaim to you what we have seen and heard, so
that you also may have fellowship with us. And our
fellowship is with the Father and with his Son, Jesus
Christ.

## HOSEA 11:4

I led them with cords of human kindness,
with ties of love;
I lifted the yoke from their neck
and bent down to feed them.

## 1 PETER 5:7

Cast all your anxiety on him because he cares for you.

## JEREMIAH 15:15

You understand, O LORD;
remember me and care for me.

# Fruitfulness

**EPHESIANS 5:9**
The fruit of the light consists in all goodness, righteousness and truth.

**GALATIANS 5:22-23**
The fruit of the Spirit is love, joy, peace, patience, kindness, goodness, faithfulness, gentleness and self-control. Against such things there is no law.

**ROMANS 7:4**
So, my brothers, you also died to the law through the body of Christ, that you might belong to another, to him who was raised from the dead, in order that we might bear fruit to God.

**JOHN 15:16**
I chose you and appointed you to go and bear fruit—fruit that will last. Then the Father will give you whatever you ask in my name.

**JOHN 15:8**
This is to my Father's glory, that you bear much fruit, showing yourselves to be my disciples.

## MATTHEW 13:23

The one who received the seed that fell on good soil is the man who hears the word and understands it. He produces a crop, yielding a hundred, sixty or thirty times what was sown.

## JOHN 12:24

I tell you the truth, unless a kernel of wheat falls to the ground and dies, it remains only a single seed. But if it dies, it produces many seeds.

## JOHN 15:5

I am the vine; you are the branches. If a man remains in me and I in him, he will bear much fruit; apart from me you can do nothing.

## MATTHEW 3:8

Produce fruit in keeping with repentance.

## JOHN 15:2

He cuts off every branch in me that bears no fruit, while every branch that does bear fruit he prunes so that it will be even more fruitful.

# Future

**1 CORINTHIANS 2:9-10**
As it is written:
"No eye has seen,
no ear has heard,
no mind has conceived
what God has prepared for those who love
him"—
but God has revealed it to us by his Spirit.
The Spirit searches all things, even the deep
things of God.

**PHILIPPIANS 3:20-21**
Our citizenship is in heaven. And we eagerly await a
Savior from there, the Lord Jesus Christ, who, by the
power that enables him to bring everything under his
control, will transform our lowly bodies so that they
will be like his glorious body.

**1 CORINTHIANS 15:51-52**
Listen, I tell you a mystery: We will not all sleep, but
we will all be changed—in a flash, in the twinkling of
an eye, at the last trumpet. For the trumpet will
sound, the dead will be raised imperishable, and we
will be changed.

### 1 JOHN 3:2

Dear friends, now we are children of God, and what we will be has not yet been made known. But we know that when he appears, we shall be like him, for we shall see him as he is.

### JEREMIAH 29:11

"For I know the plans I have for you," declares the LORD, "plans to prosper you and not to harm you, plans to give you hope and a future."

### PSALM 33:11

The plans of the LORD stand firm forever,
the purposes of his heart through all
generations.

### LUKE 12:37

It will be good for those servants whose master finds them watching when he comes. I tell you the truth, he will dress himself to serve, will have them recline at the table and will come and wait on them.

### JAMES 4:14-15

Why, you do not even know what will happen tomorrow. What is your life? You are a mist that appears for a little while and then vanishes. Instead, you ought to say, "If it is the Lord's will, we will live and do this or that."

# Generosity

**LUKE 6:30**
Give to everyone who asks you, and if anyone takes what belongs to you, do not demand it back.

**2 CORINTHIANS 9:7**
Each man should give what he has decided in his heart to give, not reluctantly or under compulsion, for God loves a cheerful giver.

**2 CORINTHIANS 9:6**
Remember this: Whoever sows sparingly will also reap sparingly, and whoever sows generously will also reap generously.

**PSALM 112:5**
Good will come to him who is generous and lends
      freely,
   who conducts his affairs with justice.

**PROVERBS 11:25**
A generous man will prosper;
   he who refreshes others will himself be
      refreshed.

**LUKE 6:38**

Give, and it will be given to you. A good measure,
pressed down, shaken together and running over, will
be poured into your lap. For with the measure you
use, it will be measured to you.

**PROVERBS 22:9**

A generous man will himself be blessed,
for he shares his food with the poor.

**PSALM 37:25-26**

I was young and now I am old,
yet I have never seen the righteous forsaken
or their children begging bread.
They are always generous and lend freely;
their children will be blessed.

**1 TIMOTHY 6:18-19**

Command them to do good, to be rich in good
deeds, and to be generous and willing to share. In this
way they will lay up treasure for themselves as a firm
foundation for the coming age, so that they may take
hold of the life that is truly life.

# Gentleness

**MATTHEW 11:29**
Take my yoke upon you and learn from me, for I am gentle and humble in heart, and you will find rest for your souls.

**COLOSSIANS 3:12**
As God's chosen people, holy and dearly loved, clothe yourselves with compassion, kindness, humility, gentleness and patience.

**1 PETER 3:3-4**
Your beauty ... should be that of your inner self, the unfading beauty of a gentle and quiet spirit, which is of great worth in God's sight.

**1 TIMOTHY 6:11**
You, man of God ... pursue righteousness, godliness, faith, love, endurance and gentleness.

**EPHESIANS 4:2**
Be completely humble and gentle; be patient, bearing with one another in love.

**PHILIPPIANS 4:5**
Let your gentleness be evident to all. The Lord is near.

**1 PETER 3:15**
In your hearts set apart Christ as Lord. Always be prepared to give an answer to everyone who asks you to give the reason for the hope that you have. But do this with gentleness and respect.

**PROVERBS 15:1**
A gentle answer turns away wrath.

**PSALM 37:11**
The meek will inherit the land
and enjoy great peace.

# Giving

## 2 CORINTHIANS 9:7

Each man should give what he has decided in his
heart to give, not reluctantly or under compulsion,
for God loves a cheerful giver.

## LUKE 6:38

Give, and it will be given to you. A good measure,
pressed down, shaken together and running over, will
be poured into your lap. For with the measure you
use, it will be measured to you.

## MALACHI 3:10

"Bring the whole tithe into the storehouse, that there
may be food in my house. Test me in this," says the
LORD Almighty, "and see if I will not throw open the
floodgates of heaven and pour out so much blessing
that you will not have room enough for it."

## ACTS 20:35

In everything I did, I showed you that by this kind of
hard work we must help the weak, remembering the

words the Lord Jesus himself said: "It is more blessed
to give than to receive."

**PROVERBS 25:21**
> If your enemy is hungry, give him food to eat;
> if he is thirsty, give him water to drink.

**PROVERBS 28:27**
> He who gives to the poor will lack nothing,
> but he who closes his eyes to them receives
> many curses.

**LUKE 6:30**
Give to everyone who asks you, and if anyone takes
what belongs to you, do not demand it back.

**LUKE 11:13**
If you then, though you are evil, know how to give
good gifts to your children, how much more will your
Father in heaven give the Holy Spirit to those who
ask him!

# Goals

**2 CORINTHIANS 5:9**
We make it our goal to please him, whether we are at home in the body or away from it.

**PHILIPPIANS 3:14**
I press on toward the goal to win the prize for which God has called me heavenward in Christ Jesus.

**1 CORINTHIANS 9:24**
Do you not know that in a race all the runners run, but only one gets the prize? Run in such a way as to get the prize.

**PHILIPPIANS 3:13-14**
Brothers, I do not consider myself yet to have taken hold of it. But one thing I do: Forgetting what is behind and straining toward what is ahead, I press on toward the goal to win the prize for which God has called me heavenward in Christ Jesus.

## 2 TIMOTHY 2:15

Do your best to present yourself to God as one
approved, a workman who does not need to be
ashamed and who correctly handles the word of
truth.

## 1 CORINTHIANS 14:1

Follow the way of love and eagerly desire spiritual
gifts, especially the gift of prophecy.

## 1 CORINTHIANS 12:31

Eagerly desire the greater gifts.

## 1 CORINTHIANS 14:12

Since you are eager to have spiritual gifts, try to excel
in gifts that build up the church.

## 1 THESSALONIANS 4:11

Make it your ambition to lead a quiet life, to mind
your own business and to work with your hands, just
as we told you.

# Good News

## 1 PETER 1:3

Praise be to the God and Father of our Lord Jesus
Christ! In his great mercy he has given us new birth
into a living hope through the resurrection of Jesus
Christ from the dead.

## JOHN 3:16

For God so loved the world that he gave his one and
only Son, that whoever believes in him shall not perish but have eternal life.

## JOHN 3:36

Whoever believes in the Son has eternal life.

## COLOSSIANS 1:19-20

For God was pleased to have all his fullness dwell in
him, and through him to reconcile to himself all
things, whether things on earth or things in heaven,
by making peace through his blood, shed on the
cross.

## ROMANS 5:8

God demonstrates his own love for us in this: While
we were still sinners, Christ died for us.

### 1 JOHN 4:10

This is love: not that we loved God, but that he loved us and sent his Son as an atoning sacrifice for our sins.

### ROMANS 5:17

For if, by the trespass of the one man, death reigned through that one man, how much more will those who receive God's abundant provision of grace and of the gift of righteousness reign in life through the one man, Jesus Christ.

### 2 CORINTHIANS 5:21

God made him who had no sin to be sin for us, so that in him we might become the righteousness of God.

### EPHESIANS 2:13

Now in Christ Jesus you who once were far away have been brought near through the blood of Christ.

### COLOSSIANS 2:13-14

When you were dead in your sins and in the uncircumcision of your sinful nature, God made you alive with Christ. He forgave us all our sins, having canceled the written code, with its regulations, that was against us and that stood opposed to us; he took it away, nailing it to the cross.

# Goodness

**JAMES 3:13**

Who is wise and understanding among you? Let him show it by his good life, by deeds done in the humility that comes from wisdom.

**1 THESSALONIANS 5:21-22**

Test everything. Hold on to the good. Avoid every kind of evil.

**PSALM 37:3**

Trust in the LORD and do good;
dwell in the land and enjoy safe pasture.

**3 JOHN 1:11**

Anyone who does what is good is from God.

**EPHESIANS 2:10**

For we are God's workmanship, created in Christ Jesus to do good works, which God prepared in advance for us to do.

## MATTHEW 5:16

Let your light shine before men, that they may see your good deeds and praise your Father in heaven.

## GALATIANS 6:10

As we have opportunity, let us do good to all people, especially to those who belong to the family of believers.

## GALATIANS 6:9

Let us not become weary in doing good, for at the proper time we will reap a harvest if we do not give up.

## ECCLESIASTES 3:12

I know that there is nothing better for men than to be happy and do good while they live.

## PROVERBS 12:2

A good man obtains favor from the LORD,
but the LORD condemns a crafty man.

## PSALM 37:27

Turn from evil and do good;
then you will dwell in the land forever.

# Goodness of God

**PSALM 145:9**

The LORD is good to all;
he has compassion on all he has made.

**PSALM 25:8**

Good and upright is the LORD;
therefore he instructs sinners in his ways.

**NAHUM 1:7**

The LORD is good,
a refuge in times of trouble.
He cares for those who trust in him.

**PSALM 31:19**

How great is your goodness,
which you have stored up for those who fear
you,
which you bestow in the sight of men
on those who take refuge in you.

## LAMENTATIONS 3:25

The LORD is good to those whose hope is in him,
to the one who seeks him.

## PSALM 27:13

I am still confident of this:
I will see the goodness of the LORD
in the land of the living.

## 2 PETER 1:3

His divine power has given us everything we need for
life and godliness through our knowledge of him who
called us by his own glory and goodness.

## PSALM 16:2

I said to the LORD, "You are my Lord;
apart from you I have no good thing."

## ROMANS 8:28

We know that in all things God works for the good
of those who love him, who have been called according to his purpose.

# Grace

**PSALM 116:5**

The LORD is gracious and righteous;
our God is full of compassion.

**LAMENTATIONS 3:22**

Because of the LORD's great love we are not
consumed,
for his compassions never fail.

**EPHESIANS 2:6-7**

God raised us up with Christ and seated us with him
in the heavenly realms in Christ Jesus, in order that in
the coming ages he might show the incomparable
riches of his grace, expressed in his kindness to us in
Christ Jesus.

**ROMANS 5:1-2**

Since we have been justified through faith, we have
peace with God through our Lord Jesus Christ,
through whom we have gained access by faith into
this grace in which we now stand. And we rejoice in
the hope of the glory of God.

## ROMANS 5:17

For if, by the trespass of the one man, death reigned through that one man, how much more will those who receive God's abundant provision of grace and of the gift of righteousness reign in life through the one man, Jesus Christ.

## 2 CORINTHIANS 8:9

For you know the grace of our Lord Jesus Christ, that though he was rich, yet for your sakes he became poor, so that you through his poverty might become rich.

## JOHN 1:16

From the fullness of his grace we have all received one blessing after another.

## 2 CORINTHIANS 9:8

God is able to make all grace abound to you, so that in all things at all times, having all that you need, you will abound in every good work.

## 2 CORINTHIANS 12:9

He said to me, "My grace is sufficient for you, for my power is made perfect in weakness." Therefore I will boast all the more gladly about my weaknesses, so that Christ's power may rest on me.

## PETER 5:10

The God of all grace, who called you to his eternal glory in Christ, after you have suffered a little while, will himself restore you and make you strong, firm and steadfast.

## 2 PETER 1:2

Grace and peace be yours in abundance through the knowledge of God and of Jesus our Lord.

## EPHESIANS 2:4-5

But because of his great love for us, God, who is rich in mercy, made us alive with Christ even when we were dead in transgressions—it is by grace you have been saved.

## 2 TIMOTHY 1:8-10

So do not be ashamed to testify about our Lord, or ashamed of me his prisoner. But join with me in suffering for the gospel, by the power of God, who has saved us and called us to a holy life—not because of anything we have done but because of his own purpose and grace. This grace was given us in Christ Jesus before the beginning of time, but it has now been revealed through the appearing of our Savior, Christ Jesus, who has destroyed death and has brought life and immortality to light through the gospel.

## TITUS 3:5-7

He saved us, not because of righteous things we had done, but because of his mercy. He saved us through the washing of rebirth and renewal by the Holy Spirit, whom he poured out on us generously through Jesus Christ our Savior, so that, having been justified by his grace, we might become heirs having the hope of eternal life.

# Growth

**PHILIPPIANS 1:9**
This is my prayer: that your love may abound more and more in knowledge and depth of insight.

**COLOSSIANS 1:10**
We pray ... in order that you may live a life worthy of the Lord and may please him in every way: bearing fruit in every good work, growing in the knowledge of God.

**1 THESSALONIANS 4:1**
Finally, brothers, we instructed you how to live in order to please God, as in fact you are living. Now we ask you and urge you in the Lord Jesus to do this more and more.

**2 PETER 1:5-6**
Make every effort to add to your faith goodness; and to goodness, knowledge; and to knowledge, self-control; and to self-control, perseverance; and to perseverance, godliness.

### 2 PETER 3:18

Grow in the grace and knowledge of our Lord and
Savior Jesus Christ. To him be glory both now and
forever! Amen.

### 1 TIMOTHY 4:15

Be diligent in these matters; give yourself wholly to
them, so that everyone may see your progress.

### 2 CORINTHIANS 3:18

We, who with unveiled faces all reflect the Lord's
glory, are being transformed into his likeness with
ever-increasing glory, which comes from the Lord,
who is the Spirit.

### PROVERBS 4:18

The path of the righteous is like the first gleam of
    dawn,
    shining ever brighter till the full light of day.

### 2 THESSALONIANS 1:3

We ought always to thank God for you, brothers, and
rightly so, because your faith is growing more and
more, and the love every one of you has for each
other is increasing.

# Guidance

**EXODUS 15:13**

In your unfailing love you will lead
   the people you have redeemed.
In your strength you will guide them
   to your holy dwelling.

**PSALM 48:14**

For this God is our God for ever and ever;
   he will be our guide even to the end.

**PSALM 23:2-3**

He makes me lie down in green pastures,
he leads me beside quiet waters,
   he restores my soul.
He guides me in paths of righteousness
   for his name's sake.

**ISAIAH 58:11**

The LORD will guide you always;
   he will satisfy your needs in a sun-scorched land
   and will strengthen your frame.

You will be like a well-watered garden,
   like a spring whose waters never fail.

**PSALM 139:9-10**
   If I rise on the wings of the dawn,
      if I settle on the far side of the sea,
   even there your hand will guide me,
      your right hand will hold me fast.

**PSALM 37:23-24**
   If the LORD delights in a man's way,
      he makes his steps firm;
   though he stumble, he will not fall,
      for the LORD upholds him with his hand.

**PROVERBS 3:5-6**
   Trust in the LORD with all your heart
      and lean not on your own understanding;
   in all your ways acknowledge him,
      and he will make your paths straight.

**ISAIAH 42:16**
   I will lead the blind by ways they have not known,
      along unfamiliar paths I will guide them;

I will turn the darkness into light before them
and make the rough places smooth.
These are the things I will do;
I will not forsake them.

## JOHN 16:13

When he, the Spirit of truth, comes, he will guide
you into all truth. He will not speak on his own; he
will speak only what he hears, and he will tell you
what is yet to come.

## JOHN 14:26

The Counselor, the Holy Spirit, whom the Father will
send in my name, will teach you all things and will
remind you of everything I have said to you.

## PSALM 107:30-32

They were glad when it grew calm,
and he guided them to their desired haven.
Let them give thanks to the LORD for his unfailing
love
and his wonderful deeds for men.
Let them exalt him in the assembly of the people
and praise him in the council of the elders.

**JEREMIAH 29:11**

"For I know the plans I have for you," declares the
LORD, "plans to prosper you and not to harm you,
plans to give you hope and a future."

**PROVERBS 4:11**

I guide you in the way of wisdom
    and lead you along straight paths.

**PROVERBS 6:20-23**

My son, keep your father's commands
    and do not forsake your mother's teaching.
Bind them upon your heart forever;
    fasten them around your neck.
When you walk, they will guide you;
    when you sleep, they will watch over you;
    when you awake, they will speak to you.
For these commands are a lamp,
    this teaching is a light,
and the corrections of discipline
    are the way to life,

# Healing

**JEREMIAH 33:6**
I will heal my people and will let them enjoy abundant peace and security.

**HOSEA 14:4**
I will heal their waywardness
and love them freely,
for my anger has turned away from them.

**1 PETER 2:24**
He himself bore our sins in his body on the tree, so that we might die to sins and live for righteousness; by his wounds you have been healed.

**PSALM 103:2-3**
Praise the LORD, O my soul,
and forget not all his benefits—
who forgives all your sins

and heals all your diseases.

**JEREMIAH 30:17**
I will restore you to health
and heal your wounds,'
declares the LORD,
'because you are called an outcast,
Zion for whom no one cares.'

**JEREMIAH 17:14**
Heal me, O LORD, and I will be healed;
save me and I will be saved,
for you are the one I praise.

**JAMES 5:15-16**
The prayer offered in faith will make the sick person
well; the Lord will raise him up. If he has sinned, he
will be forgiven. Confess your sins to each other and
pray for each other so that you may be healed. The
prayer of a righteous man is powerful and effective.

**PSALM 30:2**
O LORD my God, I called to you for help
and you healed me.

# Heaven

**REVELATION 22:14**

Blessed are those who wash their robes, that they may have the right to the tree of life and may go through the gates into the city.

**JOHN 14:2**

In my Father's house are many rooms; if it were not so, I would have told you. I am going there to prepare a place for you.

**2 CORINTHIANS 5:1**

Now we know that if the earthly tent we live in is destroyed, we have a building from God, an eternal house in heaven, not built by human hands.

## REVELATION 21:27

Nothing impure will ever enter it, nor will anyone
who does what is shameful or deceitful, but only
those whose names are written in the Lamb's book
of life.

## LUKE 10:20

Rejoice that your names are written in heaven.

## REVELATION 21:4

He will wipe every tear from their eyes. There will be
no more death or mourning or crying or pain, for the
old order of things has passed away.

## REVELATION 7:16-17

Never again will they hunger;
    never again will they thirst.
The sun will not beat upon them,
    nor any scorching heat.

For the Lamb at the center of the throne will be
their shepherd;
he will lead them to springs of living water.
And God will wipe away every tear from their
eyes.

### DANIEL 7:10

A river of fire was flowing,
coming out from before him.
Thousands upon thousands attended him;
ten thousand times ten thousand stood before
him.
The court was seated,
and the books were opened.

### REVELATION 7:9

I looked and there before me was a great multitude
that no one could count, from every nation, tribe,
people and language, standing before the throne and
in front of the Lamb. They were wearing white robes
and were holding palm branches in their hands.

## REVELATION 19:6

I heard what sounded like a great multitude, like the roar of rushing waters and like loud peals of thunder, shouting:

"Hallelujah!

For our Lord God Almighty reigns."

## PHILLIPIANS 3:20

But our citizenship is in heaven. And we eagerly await a Savior from there, the Lord Jesus Christ,

## 1 THESSALONIANS 4:15-18

According to the Lord's own word, we tell you that we who are still alive, who are left till the coming of the Lord, will certainly not precede those who have fallen asleep. For the Lord himself will come down from heaven, with a loud command, with the voice of the archangel and with the trumpet call of God, and the dead in Christ will rise first. After that, we who are still alive and are left will be caught up together with them in the clouds to meet the Lord in the air. And so we will be with the Lord forever. Therefore encourage each other with these words.

# Help

**HEBREWS 2:18**
Because he himself suffered when he was tempted, he is able to help those who are being tempted.

**PSALM 72:12**
For he will deliver the needy who cry out,
the afflicted who have no one to help.

**PSALM 10:14**
You, O God, do see trouble and grief;
you consider it to take it in hand.
The victim commits himself to you;
you are the helper of the fatherless.

**ISAIAH 59:1**
Surely the arm of the LORD is not too short
to save,
nor his ear too dull to hear.

**PSALM 46:1**
God is our refuge and strength,
an ever-present help in trouble.

PSALM 28:7

The LORD is my strength and my shield;
    my heart trusts in him, and I am helped.
My heart leaps for joy
    and I will give thanks to him in song.

PSALM 68:19

Praise be to the Lord, to God our Savior,
who daily bears our burdens.

ISAIAH 50:9

It is the Sovereign LORD who helps me.
    Who is he that will condemn me?
They will all wear out like a garment;
    the moths will eat them up.

HEBREWS 13:6

So we say with confidence,
"The Lord is my helper; I will not be afraid.
    What can man do to me?"

# Holiness

**1 THESSALONIANS 5:23**
May God himself, the God of peace, sanctify you through and through. May your whole spirit, soul and body be kept blameless at the coming of our Lord Jesus Christ.

**1 PETER 1:15-16**
Just as he who called you is holy, so be holy in all you do; for it is written: "Be holy, because I am holy."

**1 THESSALONIANS 4:7**
God did not call us to be impure, but to live a holy life.

**EPHESIANS 1:4-6**
He chose us in him before the creation of the world to be holy and blameless in his sight. In love he predestined us to be adopted as his sons through Jesus Christ, in accordance with his pleasure and will—to the praise of his glorious grace, which he has freely given us in the One he loves.

## 2 CORINTHIANS 7:1

Since we have these promises, dear friends, let us
purify ourselves from everything that contaminates
body and spirit, perfecting holiness out of reverence
for God.

## ROMANS 6:22

Now that you have been set free from sin and have
become slaves to God, the benefit you reap leads to
holiness, and the result is eternal life.

## PSALM 84:11

For the LORD God is a sun and shield;
the LORD bestows favor and honor;
no good thing does he withhold
from those whose walk is blameless.

## PSALM 119:1

Blessed are they whose ways are blameless,
who walk according to the law of the LORD.

## PROVERBS 11:5

The righteousness of the blameless makes a
straight way for them,
but the wicked are brought down by their own
wickedness.

# Honesty

**PSALM 51:6**

Surely you desire truth in the inner parts;
 you teach me wisdom in the inmost place.

**1 CORINTHIANS 13:6**

Love ... rejoices with the truth.

**EPHESIANS 6:14**

Stand firm then, with the belt of truth buckled
around your waist, with the breastplate of righteousness in place.

**TITUS 2:7-8**

In everything set them an example by doing what is
good. In your teaching show integrity, seriousness and
soundness of speech that cannot be condemned, so
that those who oppose you may be ashamed because
they have nothing bad to say about us.

**PROVERBS 10:9**

The man of integrity walks securely,
 but he who takes crooked paths will be found
 out.

**PROVERBS 13:5**
The righteous hate what is false.

**PSALM 15:2, 5**
He whose walk is blameless
and who does what is righteous,
who speaks the truth from his heart ...
He who does these things
will never be shaken.

**ISAIAH 33:15-16**
He who walks righteously
and speaks what is right ...
this is the man who will dwell on the heights,
whose refuge will be the mountain fortress.
His bread will be supplied,
and water will not fail him.

**PROVERBS 24:26**
An honest answer
is like a kiss on the lips.

# Hope

### 1 TIMOTHY 4:9-10

This is a trustworthy saying that deserves full acceptance (and for this we labor and strive), that we have put our hope in the living God, who is the Savior of all men, and especially of those who believe.

### 1 PETER 1:3

Praise be to the God and Father of our Lord Jesus Christ! In his great mercy he has given us new birth into a living hope through the resurrection of Jesus Christ from the dead.

### 1 PETER 1:21

Through him you believe in God, who raised him from the dead and glorified him, and so your faith and hope are in God.

### ACTS 2:26-27

My heart is glad and my tongue rejoices;
  my body also will live in hope,
because you will not abandon me to the grave,
  nor will you let your Holy One see decay.

**LAMENTATIONS 3:21-22**

This I call to mind
and therefore I have hope:
Because of the LORD's great love we are not
consumed,
for his compassions never fail.

**PSALM 147:11**

The LORD delights in those who fear him,
who put their hope in his unfailing love.

**LAMENTATIONS 3:25-26**

The LORD is good to those whose hope is in him,
to the one who seeks him;
it is good to wait quietly
for the salvation of the LORD.

**ROMANS 5:5**

Hope does not disappoint us, because God has
poured out his love into our hearts by the Holy
Spirit, whom he has given us.

ISAIAH 40:31

Those who hope in the LORD
    will renew their strength.
They will soar on wings like eagles;
    they will run and not grow weary,
    they will walk and not be faint.

PROVERBS 24:14

Know also that wisdom is sweet to your soul;
    if you find it, there is a future hope for you,
    and your hope will not be cut off.

PSALM 42:5-11

Why are you downcast, O my soul?
    Why so disturbed within me?
Put your hope in God,
    for I will yet praise him,
    my Savior and my God.
My soul is downcast within me;
    therefore I will remember you
from the land of the Jordan,
    the heights of Hermon—from Mount Mizar.
Deep calls to deep
    in the roar of your waterfalls;

all your waves and breakers
    have swept over me.
By day the LORD directs his love,
    at night his song is with me—
    a prayer to the God of my life.
I say to God my Rock,
    "Why have you forgotten me?
Why must I go about mourning,
    oppressed by the enemy?"
My bones suffer mortal agony
    as my foes taunt me,
saying to me all day long,
    "Where is your God?"
Why are you downcast, O my soul?
    Why so disturbed within me?
Put your hope in God,
    for I will yet praise him,
    my Savior and my God.

## JEREMIAH 29:11

For I know the plans I have for you," declares the
LORD, "plans to prosper you and not to harm you,
plans to give you hope and a future.

# Hospitality

**1 PETER 4:9**
Offer hospitality to one another without grumbling.

**TITUS 1:8**
He must be hospitable, one who loves what is good, who is self-controlled, upright, holy and disciplined.

**ROMANS 12:13**
Share with God's people who are in need. Practice hospitality.

**DEUTERONOMY 15:11**
There will always be poor people in the land. Therefore I command you to be openhanded toward your brothers and toward the poor and needy in your land.

**HEBREWS 13:2-3**
Do not forget to entertain strangers, for by so doing some people have entertained angels without knowing it. Remember those in prison as if you were their

fellow prisoners, and those who are mistreated as if you yourselves were suffering.

### MATTHEW 10:42
If anyone gives even a cup of cold water to one of these little ones because he is my disciple, I tell you the truth, he will certainly not lose his reward.

### MATTHEW 25:34-36
The King will say to those on his right, "Come, you who are blessed by my Father; take your inheritance, the kingdom prepared for you since the creation of the world. For I was hungry and you gave me something to eat, I was thirsty and you gave me something to drink, I was a stranger and you invited me in, I needed clothes and you clothed me, I was sick and you looked after me, I was in prison and you came to visit me."

### 1 PETER 4:11
If anyone speaks, he should do it as one speaking the very words of God. If anyone serves, he should do it with the strength God provides, so that in all things God may be praised through Jesus Christ. To him be the glory and the power for ever and ever. Amen.

# Humility

**PROVERBS 22:4**

> Humility and the fear of the LORD
> bring wealth and honor and life.

**JAMES 4:10**

Humble yourselves before the Lord, and he will lift
you up.

**PSALM 149:4**

> For the LORD takes delight in his people;
> he crowns the humble with salvation.

**PROVERBS 15:33**

> The fear of the LORD teaches a man wisdom,
> and humility comes before honor.

**PSALM 147:6**

> The LORD sustains the humble
> but casts the wicked to the ground.

**PSALM 25:9**

He guides the humble in what is right
and teaches them his way.

**JAMES 3:13**

Who is wise and understanding among you? Let him
show it by his good life, by deeds done in the humility that comes from wisdom.

**MATTHEW 18:4**

Whoever humbles himself like this child is the great-
est in the kingdom of heaven.

**PHILIPPIANS 2:3**

Do nothing out of selfish ambition or vain conceit,
but in humility consider others better than yourselves.

**TITUS 3:1-2**

Remind the people to be subject to rulers and authorities, to be obedient, to be ready to do whatever is
good, to slander no one, to be peaceable and considerate, and to show true humility toward all men.

# Husbands

**EPHESIANS 5:25-28**
Husbands, love your wives, just as Christ loved the church and gave himself up for her to make her holy, cleansing her by the washing with water through the word, and to present her to himself as a radiant church, without stain or wrinkle or any other blemish, but holy and blameless. In this same way, husbands ought to love their wives as their own bodies. He who loves his wife loves himself.

**1 PETER 3:7**
Husbands, in the same way be considerate as you live with your wives, and treat them with respect as the weaker partner and as heirs with you of the gracious gift of life, so that nothing will hinder your prayers.

**1 CORINTHIANS 7:4**
The wife's body does not belong to her alone but also to her husband. In the same way, the husband's body does not belong to him alone but also to his wife.

## COLOSSIANS 3:19

Husbands, love your wives and do not be harsh with them.

## PROVERBS 5:18-19

May your fountain be blessed,
    and may you rejoice in the wife of your youth.
A loving doe, a graceful deer—
    may her breasts satisfy you always,
    may you ever be captivated by her love.

## ECCLESIASTES 9:9

Enjoy life with your wife, whom you love, all the days of this meaningless life that God has given you under the sun—all your meaningless days. For this is your lot in life and in your toilsome labor under the sun.

## 1 TIMOTHY 3:2

Now the overseer must be above reproach, the husband of but one wife, temperate, self-controlled, respectable, hospitable, able to teach, not given to drunkenness, not violent but gentle, not quarrelsome, not a lover of money. He must manage his own household well and see that his children obey him with proper respect.

# Identity

**ISAIAH 43:1**

Now, this is what the LORD says—
he who created you, O Jacob,
he who formed you, O Israel:
"Fear not, for I have redeemed you;
I have summoned you by name; you are mine."

**PSALM 100:3**

Know that the LORD is God.
It is he who made us, and we are his;
we are his people, the sheep of his pasture.

**I SAMUEL 12:22**

For the sake of his great name the LORD will not
reject his people, because the LORD was pleased to
make you his own.

**I PETER 2:9**

You are a chosen people, a royal priesthood, a holy
nation, a people belonging to God, that you may
declare the praises of him who called you out of darkness into his wonderful light.

**PSALM 95:6-7**

Come, let us bow down in worship,
    let us kneel before the LORD our Maker;
for he is our God
    and we are the people of his pasture,
the flock under his care.

**EPHESIANS 1:13**

You also were included in Christ when you heard the
word of truth, the gospel of your salvation. Having
believed, you were marked in him with a seal, the
promised Holy Spirit.

**EPHESIANS 2:10**

For we are God's workmanship, created in Christ
Jesus to do good works, which God prepared in
advance for us to do.

**COLOSSIANS 3:12**

As God's chosen people, holy and dearly loved, clothe
yourselves with compassion, kindness, humility, gentleness and patience.

# Integrity

**1 CHRONICLES 29:17**
I know, my God, that you test the heart and are
pleased with integrity.

**PSALM 84:11**
For the LORD God is a sun and shield;
the LORD bestows favor and honor;
no good thing does he withhold
from those whose walk is blameless.

**PROVERBS 2:7-8**
He holds victory in store for the upright,
he is a shield to those whose walk is blameless,
for he guards the course of the just
and protects the way of his faithful ones.

**PROVERBS 10:9**
The man of integrity walks securely,
but he who takes crooked paths will be found out.

**PROVERBS 11:3**
> The integrity of the upright guides them,
>> but the unfaithful are destroyed by their
>> duplicity.

**LUKE 16:10**
Whoever can be trusted with very little can also be trusted with much, and whoever is dishonest with very little will also be dishonest with much.

**ISAIAH 57:2**
> Those who walk uprightly
>> enter into peace;
>> they find rest as they lie in death.

**PROVERBS 16:7**
> When a man's ways are pleasing to the LORD,
>> he makes even his enemies live at peace with
>> him.

**JAMES 2:18**
Someone will say, "You have faith; I have deeds."
Show me your faith without deeds, and I will show you my faith by what I do.

# Joy

**PSALM 19:8**

The precepts of the LORD are right,
giving joy to the heart.
The commands of the LORD are radiant,
giving light to the eyes.

**HEBREWS 1:9**

You have loved righteousness and hated
wickedness;
therefore God, your God, has set you above
your companions
by anointing you with the oil of joy.

**PSALM 30:11–12**

You turned my wailing into dancing;
you removed my sackcloth and clothed me
with joy,
that my heart may sing to you and not be silent.
O LORD my God, I will give you thanks
forever.

PSALM 92:4
For you make me glad by your deeds, O LORD;
I sing for joy at the works of your hands.

ISAIAH 61:10
I delight greatly in the LORD;
my soul rejoices in my God.
For he has clothed me with garments of salvation
and arrayed me in a robe of righteousness,
as a bridegroom adorns his head like a priest,
and as a bride adorns herself with her jewels.

PSALM 16:11
You have made known to me the path of life;
you will fill me with joy in your presence,
with eternal pleasures at your right hand.

PSALM 21:6
Surely you have granted him eternal blessings
and made him glad with the joy of your
presence.

## I PETER 1:8-9
Though you have not seen him, you love him; and even though you do not see him now, you believe in him and are filled with an inexpressible and glorious joy, for you are receiving the goal of your faith, the salvation of your souls.

## JAMES 1:2-3
Consider it pure joy, my brothers, whenever you face trials of many kinds, because you know that the testing of your faith develops perseverance.

## JOHN 16:24
Until now you have not asked for anything in my name. Ask and you will receive, and your joy will be complete.

## DEUTERONOMY 16:15
For seven days celebrate the Feast to the LORD your God at the place the LORD will choose. For the LORD your God will bless you in all your harvest and in all the work of your hands, and your joy will be complete.

1 CHRONICLES 16:30-33

Tremble before him, all the earth!
The world is firmly established; it cannot be
moved.
Let the heavens rejoice, let the earth be glad;
let them say among the nations, "The LORD
reigns!"
Let the sea resound, and all that is in it;
let the fields be jubilant, and everything in
them!
Then the trees of the forest will sing,
they will sing for joy before the LORD,
for he comes to judge the earth.

ACTS 2:26-28

Therefore my heart is glad and my tongue rejoices;
my body also will live in hope,
because you will not abandon me to the grave,
nor will you let your Holy One see decay.
You have made known to me the paths of life;
you will fill me with joy in your presence.

# Justice

**MICAH 6:8**

He has showed you, O man, what is good.
  And what does the LORD require of you?
To act justly and to love mercy
  and to walk humbly with your God.

**ROMANS 2:13**

For it is not those who hear the law who are righteous
in God's sight, but it is those who obey the law who
will be declared righteous.

**PSALM 37:28**

For the LORD loves the just
  and will not forsake his faithful ones.
They will be protected forever,
  but the offspring of the wicked will be cut off.

PROVERBS 2:7-8

He holds victory in store for the upright,
    he is a shield to those whose walk is blameless,
for he guards the course of the just
    and protects the way of his faithful ones.

ISAIAH 1:17

Learn to do right!
    Seek justice,
encourage the oppressed.
    Defend the cause of the fatherless,
plead the case of the widow.

PROVERBS 31:8-9

Speak up for those who cannot speak for
        themselves,
    for the rights of all who are destitute.
Speak up and judge fairly;
    defend the rights of the poor and needy.

# Justice of God

PSALM 11:7

For the LORD is righteous,
    he loves justice;
        upright men will see his face.

PSALM 103:6

The LORD works righteousness
    and justice for all the oppressed.

PSALM 111:7

The works of his hands are faithful and just;
    all his precepts are trustworthy.

EXODUS 34:6-7

The LORD, the LORD, the compassionate and gracious God, slow to anger, abounding in love and faithfulness, maintaining love to thousands, and forgiving wickedness, rebellion and sin. Yet he does not leave the guilty unpunished; he punishes the children and their children for the sin of the fathers to the third and fourth generation.

ISAIAH 30:18

Yet the LORD longs to be gracious to you;
    he rises to show you compassion.
For the LORD is a God of justice.
    Blessed are all who wait for him!

DEUTERONOMY 32:4

He is the Rock, his works are perfect,
    and all his ways are just.
A faithful God who does no wrong,
    upright and just is he.

PSALM 67:4

May the nations be glad and sing for joy,
    for you rule the peoples justly
    and guide the nations of the earth.

2 THESSALONIANS 1:5

God's judgment is right, and as a result you will be
counted worthy of the kingdom of God, for which
you are suffering.

# Justification

**GALATIANS 3:24**
The law was put in charge to lead us to Christ that
we might be justified by faith.

**2 CORINTHIANS 5:21**
God made him who had no sin to be sin for us,
so that in him we might become the righteousness
of God.

**ROMANS 5:18-19**
Just as the result of one trespass was condemnation
for all men, so also the result of one act of righteousness was justification that brings life for all men. For
just as through the disobedience of the one man the
many were made sinners, so also through the obedi-
ence of the one man the many will be made righteous.

**1 CORINTHIANS 6:11**
You were washed, you were sanctified, you were justi-
fied in the name of the Lord Jesus Christ and by the
Spirit of our God.

**GENESIS 15:6**
Abram believed the LORD, and he credited it to him
as righteousness.

**ROMANS 5:1**
Since we have been justified through faith, we have
peace with God through our Lord Jesus Christ.

**ROMANS 10:10**
For it is with your heart that you believe and are justified, and it is with your mouth that you confess and
are saved.

**JAMES 2:24**
You see that a person is justified by what he does and
not by faith alone.

**ROMANS 3:25-26**
God presented him as a sacrifice of atonement,
through faith in his blood. He did this to demonstrate his justice, because in his forbearance he had
left the sins committed beforehand unpunished— he
did it to demonstrate his justice at the present time,
so as to be just and the one who justifies those who
have faith in Jesus.

# Kindness

**PROVERBS 11:16**

A kindhearted woman gains respect,
   but ruthless men gain only wealth.

**PROVERBS 11:17**

A kind man benefits himself,
   but a cruel man brings trouble on himself.

**EPHESIANS 4:32**

Be kind and compassionate to one another, forgiving
each other, just as in Christ God forgave you.

**COLOSSIANS 3:12**

As God's chosen people, holy and dearly loved, clothe
yourselves with compassion, kindness, humility, gentleness and patience.

**2 PETER 1:5-7**

For this very reason, make every effort to add to
your faith goodness; and to goodness, knowledge;
and to knowledge, self-control; and to self-control,

perseverance; and to perseverance, godliness; and to godliness, brotherly kindness; and to brotherly kindness, love.

## MATTHEW 7:12

So in everything, do to others what you would have them do to you, for this sums up the Law and the Prophets.

## PROVERBS 14:31

Whoever is kind to the needy honors God.

## PROVERBS 19:17

He who is kind to the poor lends to the LORD,
and he will reward him for what he has done.

## 1 CORINTHIANS 13:4

Love is patient, love is kind. It does not envy, it does not boast, it is not proud.

## 1 THESSALONIANS 5:15

Make sure that nobody pays back wrong for wrong, but always try to be kind to each other and to everyone else.

# Kindness of God

**JEREMIAH 31:3**
The LORD appeared to us in the past, saying:
"I have loved you with an everlasting love;
I have drawn you with loving-kindness."

**HOSEA 11:4**
I led them with cords of human kindness,
with ties of love;
I lifted the yoke from their neck
and bent down to feed them.

**ISAIAH 63:7**
I will tell of the kindnesses of the LORD,
the deeds for which he is to be praised,
according to all the LORD has done for us—
yes, the many good things he has done
for the house of Israel,
according to his compassion and many
kindnesses.

**ROMANS 2:4**
God's kindness leads you toward repentance.

**JEREMIAH 9:24**
"Let him who boasts boast about this:
that he understands and knows me,

that I am the LORD, who exercises kindness,
  justice and righteousness on earth,
    for in these I delight,"

declares the LORD.

## JOB 10:12

You gave me life and showed me kindness,
  and in your providence watched over my spirit.

## TITUS 3:4-5

When the kindness and love of God our Savior
appeared, he saved us, not because of righteous things
we had done, but because of his mercy. He saved us
through the washing of rebirth and renewal by the
Holy Spirit.

## EPHESIANS 2:6-7

God raised us up with Christ and seated us with him
in the heavenly realms in Christ Jesus, in order that in
the coming ages he might show the incomparable
riches of his grace, expressed in his kindness to us in
Christ Jesus.

## ROMANS 11:22

Consider therefore the kindness and sternness of
God: sternness to those who fell, but kindness to you,
provided that you continue in his kindness.

# Kingdom of God

**PSALM 103:19**

The LORD has established his throne in heaven,
and his kingdom rules over all.

**PSALM 45:6**

Your throne, O God, will last for ever and ever;
a scepter of justice will be the scepter of your
kingdom.

**DANIEL 7:27**

Then the sovereignty, power and greatness of the
kingdoms under the whole heaven will be handed
over to the saints, the people of the Most High. His
kingdom will be an everlasting kingdom, and all
rulers will worship and obey him.

**JOHN 18:36**

Jesus said, "My kingdom is not of this world ... But
now my kingdom is from another place."

**LUKE 17:21**
The kingdom of God is within you.

**ROMANS 14:17**
For the kingdom of God is not a matter of eating and drinking, but of righteousness, peace and joy in the Holy Spirit.

**MATTHEW 4:17**
Repent, for the kingdom of heaven is near.

**LUKE 12:32**
Do not be afraid, little flock, for your Father has been pleased to give you the kingdom.

**COLOSSIANS 1:13-14**
For he has rescued us from the dominion of darkness and brought us into the kingdom of the Son he loves, in whom we have redemption, the forgiveness of sins.

**HEBREWS 12:28**
Since we are receiving a kingdom that cannot be shaken, let us be thankful, and so worship God acceptably with reverence and awe.

# Life

**JOHN 6:35**
Then Jesus declared, "I am the bread of life. He who comes to me will never go hungry, and he who believes in me will never be thirsty."

**JOHN 11:25-26**
Jesus said to her, "I am the resurrection and the life. He who believes in me will live, even though he dies; and whoever lives and believes in me will never die. Do you believe this?"

**ROMANS 6:11**
Count yourselves dead to sin but alive to God in Christ Jesus.

**ROMANS 8:2**
Through Christ Jesus the law of the Spirit of life set me free from the law of sin and death.

## JOHN 6:63

The Spirit gives life; the flesh counts for nothing. The words I have spoken to you are spirit and they are life.

## ROMANS 8:11

If the Spirit of him who raised Jesus from the dead is living in you, he who raised Christ from the dead will also give life to your mortal bodies through his Spirit, who lives in you.

## JOB 33:4

The Spirit of God has made me;
the breath of the Almighty gives me life.

## ACTS 2:28

You have made known to me the paths of life;
you will fill me with joy in your presence.

## PROVERBS 3:1-2

My son, do not forget my teaching,
but keep my commands in your heart,
for they will prolong your life many years
and bring you prosperity.

# Love for God

### MARK 12:29-31

"The most important one," answered Jesus, "is this: 'Hear, O Israel, the Lord our God, the Lord is one. Love the Lord your God with all your heart and with all your soul and with all your mind and with all your strength.' The second is this: 'Love your neighbor as yourself.' There is no commandment greater than these."

### MATTHEW 22:37

Jesus replied: " 'Love the Lord your God with all your heart and with all your soul and with all your mind.' "

### DEUTERONOMY 30:20

Love the LORD your God, listen to his voice, and hold fast to him. For the LORD is your life.

### PSALM 31:23

Love the LORD, all his saints!
The LORD preserves the faithful,
but the proud he pays back in full.

**1 JOHN 5:3**

This is love for God: to obey his commands. And his commands are not burdensome.

**JOHN 14:21**

Whoever has my commands and obeys them, he is the one who loves me. He who loves me will be loved by my Father, and I too will love him and show myself to him.

**JOHN 14:23**

Jesus replied, "If anyone loves me, he will obey my teaching. My Father will love him, and we will come to him and make our home with him."

**PSALM 91:14**

"Because he loves me," says the LORD, "I will
    rescue him;
    I will protect him, for he acknowledges my
        name."

# Love for Others

**JAMES 2:8**
If you really keep the royal law found in Scripture, "Love your neighbor as yourself," you are doing right.

**1 JOHN 4:19**
We love because he first loved us.

**1 JOHN 4:7**
Dear friends, let us love one another, for love comes from God. Everyone who loves has been born of God and knows God.

**COLOSSIANS 3:12-14**
As God's chosen people, holy and dearly loved, clothe yourselves with compassion, kindness, humility, gentleness and patience. Bear with each other and forgive whatever grievances you may have against one another. Forgive as the Lord forgave you. And over all these virtues put on love, which binds them all together in perfect unity.

**HEBREWS 13:1**
Keep on loving each other as brothers.

## 1 THESSALONIANS 4:9-10

Now about brotherly love we do not need to write to you, for you yourselves have been taught by God to love each other. And in fact, you do love all the brothers throughout Macedonia. Yet we urge you, brothers, to do so more and more.

## 1 JOHN 2:10

Whoever loves his brother lives in the light, and there is nothing in him to make him stumble.

## 1 JOHN 4:18

There is no fear in love. But perfect love drives out fear, because fear has to do with punishment. The one who fears is not made perfect in love.

## MATTHEW 5:44-45

I tell you: Love your enemies and pray for those who persecute you, that you may be sons of your Father in heaven.

## PROVERBS 17:9

He who covers over an offense promotes love,
but whoever repeats the matter separates close
friends.

# Love of God

**PSALM 145:8**

The LORD is gracious and compassionate,
slow to anger and rich in love.

**PSALM 107:8-9**

Let them give thanks to the LORD for his
unfailing love
and his wonderful deeds for men,
for he satisfies the thirsty
and fills the hungry with good things.

**JEREMIAH 31:3**

The LORD appeared to us in the past, saying:
"I have loved you with an everlasting love;
I have drawn you with loving-kindness."

**ISAIAH 54:10**

"Though the mountains be shaken
and the hills be removed,
yet my unfailing love for you will not be shaken
nor my covenant of peace be removed,"
says the LORD, who has compassion on you.

### PSALM 103:17

From everlasting to everlasting
    the LORD's love is with those who fear him,
    and his righteousness with their children's
        children.

### HOSEA 2:19-20

I will betroth you to me forever;
    I will betroth you in righteousness and justice,
    in love and compassion.
I will betroth you in faithfulness,
    and you will acknowledge the LORD.

### EPHESIANS 2:4-5

Because of his great love for us, God, who is rich in
mercy, made us alive with Christ even when we were
dead in transgressions—it is by grace you have been
saved.

### LAMENTATIONS 3:22-23

Because of the LORD's great love we are not
    consumed,
    for his compassions never fail.
They are new every morning;
great is your faithfulness.

# Marriage

**GENESIS 2:18**
The LORD God said, "It is not good for the man to be alone. I will make a helper suitable for him."

**ECCLESIASTES 4:9-10**
Two are better than one,
    because they have a good return for their work:
If one falls down,
    his friend can help him up.
But pity the man who falls
    and has no one to help him up!

**GENESIS 2:24**
For this reason a man will leave his father and mother and be united to his wife, and they will become one flesh.

**MARK 10:8-9**
"The two will become one flesh." So they are no longer two, but one. Therefore what God has joined together, let man not separate.

**1 CORINTHIANS 7:4**
The wife's body does not belong to her alone but also to her husband. In the same way, the husband's body does not belong to him alone but also to his wife.

## 1 CORINTHIANS 7:3

The husband should fulfill his marital duty to his
wife, and likewise the wife to her husband.

## HEBREWS 13:4

Marriage should be honored by all, and the marriage
bed kept pure, for God will judge the adulterer and
all the sexually immoral.

## PROVERBS 5:15

Drink water from your own cistern,
running water from your own well.

## SONG OF SOLOMON 8:7

Many waters cannot quench love;
rivers cannot wash it away.
If one were to give
all the wealth of his house for love,
it would be utterly scorned.

## COLOSSIANS 3:18-19

Wives, submit to your husbands, as is fitting in the
Lord.
Husbands, love your wives and do not be harsh
with them.

# Maturity

**1 PETER 2:2**
Like newborn babies, crave pure spiritual milk, so
that by it you may grow up in your salvation.

**PROVERBS 9:9**
Instruct a wise man and he will be wiser still;
    teach a righteous man and he will add to his
        learning.

**PSALM 90:12**
Teach us to number our days aright,
    that we may gain a heart of wisdom.

**ISAIAH 43:18-19**
Forget the former things;
    do not dwell on the past.
See, I am doing a new thing!
    Now it springs up; do you not perceive it?
I am making a way in the desert
    and streams in the wasteland.

**PHILIPPIANS 2:13**
It is God who works in you to will and to act according to his good purpose.

**PHILIPPIANS 1:6**
He who began a good work in you will carry it on to completion until the day of Christ Jesus.

**EPHESIANS 4:11-13**
It was he who gave some to be apostles, some to be prophets, some to be evangelists, and some to be pastors and teachers, to prepare God's people for works of service, so that the body of Christ may be built up until we all reach unity in the faith and in the knowledge of the Son of God and become mature, attaining to the whole measure of the fullness of Christ.

**JAMES 1:4**
Perseverance must finish its work so that you may be mature and complete, not lacking anything.

# Meditation

**JOSHUA 1:8**
Do not let this Book of the Law depart from your
mouth; meditate on it day and night, so that you may
be careful to do everything written in it. Then you
will be prosperous and successful.

**PSALM 1:1-2**
Blessed is the man
who does not walk in the counsel of the wicked
or stand in the way of sinners
or sit in the seat of mockers.
But his delight is in the law of the LORD,
and on his law he meditates day and night.

**PSALM 119:97**
Oh, how I love your law!
I meditate on it all day long.

**PSALM 119:147-148**
I rise before dawn and cry for help;
I have put my hope in your word.
My eyes stay open through the watches of the
night,
that I may meditate on your promises.

PSALM 119:15

I meditate on your precepts
and consider your ways.

PSALM 48:9

Within your temple, O God,
we meditate on your unfailing love.

PSALM 77:12

I will meditate on all your works
and consider all your mighty deeds.

PSALM 104:33-34

I will sing to the LORD all my life;
I will sing praise to my God as long as I live.
May my meditation be pleasing to him,
as I rejoice in the LORD.

PSALM 19:14

May the words of my mouth and the meditation
of my heart
be pleasing in your sight,
O LORD, my Rock and my Redeemer.

# Men

**1 CORINTHIANS 11:3**
Now I want you to realize that the head of every man is Christ, and the head of the woman is man, and the head of Christ is God.

**1 TIMOTHY 2:8**
I want men everywhere to lift up holy hands in prayer, without anger or disputing.

**PSALM 112:1**
Blessed is the man who fears the LORD,
who finds great delight in his commands.

**1 TIMOTHY 6:11**
You, man of God, ... pursue righteousness, godliness, faith, love, endurance and gentleness.

**PROVERBS 14:15-16**
A prudent man gives thought to his steps.
A wise man fears the LORD and shuns evil,
but a fool is hotheaded and reckless.

**PROVERBS 11:17**
A kind man benefits himself,
but a cruel man brings trouble on himself.

**PSALM 119:9**
How can a young man keep his way pure?
By living according to your word.

**TITUS 2:6**
Encourage the young men to be self-controlled.

**1 PETER 5:5**
Young men, in the same way be submissive to those
who are older. All of you, clothe yourselves with
humility toward one another, because,

"God opposes the proud
but gives grace to the humble."

**TITUS 2:2**
Teach the older men to be temperate, worthy of
respect, self-controlled, and sound in faith, in love
and in endurance.

# Mercy of God

**JAMES 5:11**
The Lord is full of compassion and mercy.

**PSALM 145:8**
The LORD is gracious and compassionate,
slow to anger and rich in love.

**ISAIAH 55:6-7**
Seek the LORD while he may be found;
call on him while he is near.
Let the wicked forsake his way
and the evil man his thoughts.
Let him turn to the LORD, and he will have mercy
on him,
and to our God, for he will freely pardon.

**ISAIAH 38:17**
Surely it was for my benefit
that I suffered such anguish.
In your love you kept me
from the pit of destruction;
you have put all my sins
behind your back.

**LAMENTATIONS 3:22-23**
Because of the LORD's great love we are not
consumed,

for his compassions never fail.
They are new every morning;
 great is your faithfulness.

PSALM 6:9
The LORD has heard my cry for mercy;
 the LORD accepts my prayer.

LUKE 1:50
His mercy extends to those who fear him,
 from generation to generation.

PSALM 5:7
I, by your great mercy,
 will come into your house;
in reverence will I bow down
 toward your holy temple.

1 PETER 1:3
Praise be to the God and Father of our Lord Jesus
Christ! In his great mercy he has given us new birth
into a living hope through the resurrection of Jesus
Christ from the dead.

TITUS 3:5
He saved us, not because of righteous things we had
done, but because of his mercy. He saved us through
the washing of rebirth and renewal by the Holy
Spirit.

# Nature

ACTS 4:24
When they heard this, they raised their voices together in prayer to God. "Sovereign Lord," they said, "you made the heaven and the earth and the sea, and everything in them."

PSALM 102:25
In the beginning you laid the foundations
of the earth,
and the heavens are the work of your hands.

NEHEMIAH 9:6
You alone are the LORD. You made the heavens, even the highest heavens, and all their starry host, the earth and all that is on it, the seas and all that is in them. You give life to everything, and the multitudes of heaven worship you.

ISAIAH 44:23
Sing for joy, O heavens, for the LORD has done
this;
shout aloud, O earth beneath.
Burst into song, you mountains,
you forests and all your trees,

for the LORD has redeemed Jacob,
   he displays his glory in Israel.

PSALM 65:13

The meadows are covered with flocks
   and the valleys are mantled with grain;
   they shout for joy and sing.

PSALM 69:34

Let heaven and earth praise him,
   the seas and all that move in them.

PSALM 44:23

Awake, O Lord! Why do you sleep?
   Rouse yourself! Do not reject us forever.

PSALM 19:1

The heavens declare the glory of God;
   the skies proclaim the work of his hands.

ECCLESIASTES 3:11

He has made everything beautiful in its time. He has
also set eternity in the hearts of men; yet they cannot
fathom what God has done from beginning to end.

JOB 26:7

He spreads out the northern skies over empty
      space;
   he suspends the earth over nothing.

# New Life

**2 CORINTHIANS 5:17**
If anyone is in Christ, he is a new creation; the old
has gone, the new has come!

**EZEKIEL 11:19**
I will give them an undivided heart and put a new
spirit in them; I will remove from them their heart of
stone and give them a heart of flesh.

**ROMANS 6:4**
We were therefore buried with him through baptism
into death in order that, just as Christ was raised
from the dead through the glory of the Father, we too
may live a new life.

**JOHN 11:25-26**
Jesus said to her, "I am the resurrection and the life.
He who believes in me will live, even though he dies;
and whoever lives and believes in me will never die.
Do you believe this?"

## EPHESIANS 2:4-5

Because of his great love for us, God, who is rich in mercy, made us alive with Christ even when we were dead in transgressions—it is by grace you have been saved.

## EZEKIEL 36:26

I will give you a new heart and put a new spirit in you; I will remove from you your heart of stone and give you a heart of flesh.

## EPHESIANS 4:24

Put on the new self, created to be like God in true righteousness and holiness.

## COLOSSIANS 3:9-10

You have taken off your old self with its practices and have put on the new self, which is being renewed in knowledge in the image of its Creator.

# Obedience

### ROMANS 2:13
For it is not those who hear the law who are righteous in God's sight, but it is those who obey the law who will be declared righteous.

### LUKE 11:28
He replied, "Blessed rather are those who hear the word of God and obey it."

### MATTHEW 7:24-25
Everyone who hears these words of mine and puts them into practice is like a wise man who built his house on the rock. The rain came down, the streams rose, and the winds blew and beat against that house; yet it did not fall, because it had its foundation on the rock.

### JAMES 1:25
The man who looks intently into the perfect law that gives freedom, and continues to do this, not forgetting what he has heard, but doing it—he will be blessed in what he does.

### MATTHEW 5:19
Whoever practices and teaches these commands will be called great in the kingdom of heaven.

### JOHN 15:10-11

If you obey my commands, you will remain in my love, just as I have obeyed my Father's commands and remain in his love. I have told you this so that my joy may be in you and that your joy may be complete.

### DEUTERONOMY 13:4

It is the LORD your God you must follow, and him you must revere. Keep his commands and obey him; serve him and hold fast to him.

### 1 JOHN 2:5

If anyone obeys his word, God's love is truly made complete in him. This is how we know we are in him.

### JOB 36:11

If they obey and serve him,
they will spend the rest of their days in
prosperity
and their years in contentment.

### DEUTERONOMY 30:16

For I command you today to love the LORD your God, to walk in his ways, and to keep his commands, decrees and laws; then you will live and increase, and the LORD your God will bless you in the land you are entering to possess.

# Parents

**PROVERBS 20:7**

The righteous man leads a blameless life;
blessed are his children after him.

**PSALM 103:17**

From everlasting to everlasting
the LORD's love is with those who fear him,
and his righteousness with their children's
children.

**DEUTERONOMY 4:40**

Keep his decrees and commands, which I am giving
you today, so that it may go well with you and your
children after you and that you may live long in the
land the LORD your God gives you for all time.

**PROVERBS 22:6**

Train a child in the way he should go,
and when he is old he will not turn from it.

**PROVERBS 29:17**

Discipline your son, and he will give you peace;
he will bring delight to your soul.

**PROVERBS 29:15**

The rod of correction imparts wisdom,
but a child left to himself disgraces his mother.

**ISAIAH 54:13**

All your sons will be taught by the LORD,
and great will be your children's peace.

**DEUTERONOMY 6:6-7**

These commandments that I give you today are to be
upon your hearts. Impress them on your children.
Talk about them when you sit at home and when you
walk along the road, when you lie down and when
you get up.

**PROVERBS 17:6**

Children's children are a crown to the aged,
and parents are the pride of their children.

**PROVERBS 13:22**

A good man leaves an inheritance for his children's
children,
but a sinner's wealth is stored up for the
righteous.

# Patience

**ROMANS 12:12**
Be joyful in hope, patient in affliction, faithful in prayer.

**PSALM 40:1**
I waited patiently for the LORD;
he turned to me and heard my cry.

**PSALM 37:7**
Be still before the LORD and wait patiently for
him;
do not fret when men succeed in their ways,
when they carry out their wicked schemes.

**COLOSSIANS 3:13**
Bear with each other and forgive whatever grievances
you may have against one another. Forgive as the
Lord forgave you.

**PROVERBS 19:11**
A man's wisdom gives him patience;
it is to his glory to overlook an offense.

**EPHESIANS 4:2**
Be completely humble and gentle; be patient, bearing with one another in love.

**PROVERBS 12:16**
A fool shows his annoyance at once,
    but a prudent man overlooks an insult.

**1 THESSALONIANS 5:14**
We urge you, brothers, warn those who are idle, encourage the timid, help the weak, be patient with everyone.

**PROVERBS 14:29**
A patient man has great understanding,
    but a quick-tempered man displays folly.

# Peace

**ROMANS 5:1**
Since we have been justified through faith, we have peace with God through our Lord Jesus Christ.

**PSALM 85:8**
I will listen to what God the LORD will say;
he promises peace to his people, his saints.

**PSALM 119:165**
Great peace have they who love your law,
and nothing can make them stumble.

**ISAIAH 26:3**
You will keep in perfect peace
him whose mind is steadfast,
because he trusts in you.

**PHILIPPIANS 4:6-7**
In everything, by prayer and petition, with thanksgiving, present your requests to God. And the peace of God, which transcends all understanding, will guard your hearts and your minds in Christ Jesus.

**ROMANS 8:6**

The mind controlled by the Spirit is life and peace.

**PROVERBS 16:7**

When a man's ways are pleasing to the LORD,
  he makes even his enemies live at peace with
    him.

**JAMES 3:18**

Peacemakers who sow in peace raise a harvest of
righteousness.

**MATTHEW 5:9**

Blessed are the peacemakers,
  for they will be called sons of God.

**2 CORINTHIANS 13:11**

Finally, brothers, good-by. Aim for perfection, listen
to my appeal, be of one mind, live in peace. And the
God of love and peace will be with you.

# Perseverance

**JAMES 1:12**
Blessed is the man who perseveres under trial, because when he has stood the test, he will receive the crown of life that God has promised to those who love him.

**1 PETER 5:10**
The God of all grace, who called you to his eternal glory in Christ, after you have suffered a little while, will himself restore you and make you strong, firm and steadfast.

**2 CORINTHIANS 4:17**
For our light and momentary troubles are achieving for us an eternal glory that far outweighs them all.

**ROMANS 2:7**
To those who by persistence in doing good seek glory, honor and immortality, he will give eternal life.

**PSALM 119:50**
My comfort in my suffering is this:
Your promise preserves my life.

**PSALM 17:5**
> My steps have held to your paths;
>> my feet have not slipped.

**JAMES 1:4-5**
Perseverance must finish its work so that you may be
mature and complete, not lacking anything.

**GALATIANS 6:9**
Let us not become weary in doing good, for at the
proper time we will reap a harvest if we do not
give up.

**PSALM 126:5**
> Those who sow in tears
>> will reap with songs of joy.

**PROVERBS 14:23**
> All hard work brings a profit,
>> but mere talk leads only to poverty.

# Praise

**1 CHRONICLES 16:25**

For great is the LORD and most worthy of praise;
he is to be feared above all gods.

**PSALM 103:2-4**

Praise the LORD, O my soul,
and forget not all his benefits—
who forgives all your sins
and heals all your diseases,
who redeems your life from the pit
and crowns you with love and compassion.

**2 SAMUEL 22:47**

The LORD lives! Praise be to my Rock!
Exalted be God, the Rock, my Savior!

**PSALM 28:6**

Praise be to the LORD,
for he has heard my cry for mercy.

1 PETER 1:3

Praise be to the God and Father of our Lord Jesus
Christ! In his great mercy he has given us new birth
into a living hope through the resurrection of Jesus
Christ from the dead.

PSALM 52:9

I will praise you forever for what you have done;
    in your name I will hope, for your name is
        good.
I will praise you in the presence of your saints.

PSALM 9:1-2

I will praise you, O LORD, with all my heart;
    I will tell of all your wonders.
I will be glad and rejoice in you;
    I will sing praise to your name, O Most High.

PSALM 139:14

I praise you because I am fearfully and wonderfully
        made;
    your works are wonderful,
    I know that full well.

# Prayer

**1 THESSALONIANS 5:17**
Pray continually.

**COLOSSIANS 4:2**
Devote yourselves to prayer, being watchful and
thankful.

**MATTHEW 26:41**
Watch and pray so that you will not fall into temptation. The spirit is willing, but the body is weak.

**EPHESIANS 6:18**
Pray in the Spirit on all occasions with all kinds of
prayers and requests. With this in mind, be alert and
always keep on praying for all the saints.

**JEREMIAH 29:12**
You will call upon me and come and pray to me, and
I will listen to you.

## DEUTERONOMY 4:7
What other nation is so great as to have their gods near them the way the LORD our God is near us whenever we pray to him?

## 2 CHRONICLES 7:14
If my people, who are called by my name, will humble themselves and pray and seek my face and turn from their wicked ways, then will I hear from heaven and will forgive their sin and will heal their land.

## JAMES 5:15
The prayer offered in faith will make the sick person well; the Lord will raise him up. If he has sinned, he will be forgiven.

## MARK 11:25
When you stand praying, if you hold anything against anyone, forgive him, so that your Father in heaven may forgive you your sins.

# Presence of God

PSALM 145:18

The LORD is near to all who call on him,
to all who call on him in truth.

ACTS 17:27

[People] reach out for [God] and find him, though he
is not far from each one of us.

PSALM 139:9-10

If I rise on the wings of the dawn,
if I settle on the far side of the sea,
even there your hand will guide me,
your right hand will hold me fast.

HEBREWS 13:5

Never will I leave you;
never will I forsake you.

PSALM 23:4

Even though I walk
through the valley of the shadow of death,
I will fear no evil,

for you are with me;
your rod and your staff,
they comfort me.

ISAIAH 43:2-3
When you pass through the waters,
I will be with you;
and when you pass through the rivers,
they will not sweep over you.
When you walk through the fire,
you will not be burned;
the flames will not set you ablaze.
For I am the LORD, your God,
the Holy One of Israel, your Savior.

DEUTERONOMY 31:6
Be strong and courageous. Do not be afraid or terri-
fied because of them, for the LORD your God goes
with you; he will never leave you nor forsake you.

EXODUS 33:14
The LORD replied, "My Presence will go with you,
and I will give you rest."

# Priorities

**MATTHEW 6:33**
Seek first his kingdom and his righteousness, and all
these things will be given to you as well.

**ECCLESIASTES 12:13**
Now all has been heard;
here is the conclusion of the matter:
Fear God and keep his commandments,
for this is the whole duty of man.

**2 CORINTHIANS 5:9**
We make it our goal to please him, whether we are at
home in the body or away from it.

**MATTHEW 6:24**
No one can serve two masters. Either he will hate the
one and love the other, or he will be devoted to the
one and despise the other. You cannot serve both God
and Money.

**PROVERBS 21:21**

He who pursues righteousness and love
    finds life, prosperity and honor.

**2 TIMOTHY 2:22**

Flee the evil desires of youth, and pursue righteousness, faith, love and peace, along with those who call on the Lord out of a pure heart.

**1 PETER 2:2**

Like newborn babies, crave pure spiritual milk, so that by it you may grow up in your salvation.

**PHILIPPIANS 3:13-14**

Brothers, I do not consider myself yet to have taken hold of it. But one thing I do: Forgetting what is behind and straining toward what is ahead, I press on toward the goal to win the prize for which God has called me heavenward in Christ Jesus.

**1 KINGS 22:5**

But Jehoshaphat also said to the king of Israel, "First seek the counsel of the LORD."

# Protection

**PSALM 55:22**

Cast your cares on the LORD
and he will sustain you;
he will never let the righteous fall.

**PSALM 145:20**

The LORD watches over all who love him,
but all the wicked he will destroy.

**PSALM 37:28**

For the LORD loves the just
and will not forsake his faithful ones.
They will be protected forever,
but the offspring of the wicked will be cut off.

**PSALM 91:14-15**

"Because he loves me," says the LORD, "I will
rescue him;
I will protect him, for he acknowledges my
name.
He will call upon me, and I will answer him;
I will be with him in trouble,
I will deliver him and honor him."

## DEUTERONOMY 33:27

The eternal God is your refuge,
and underneath are the everlasting arms.
He will drive out your enemy before you,
saying, "Destroy him!"

## 2 SAMUEL 22:31

As for God, his way is perfect;
the word of the LORD is flawless.
He is a shield
for all who take refuge in him.

## PROVERBS 2:7-8

He holds victory in store for the upright,
he is a shield to those whose walk is blameless,
for he guards the course of the just
and protects the way of his faithful ones.

## PSALM 32:7

You are my hiding place;
you will protect me from trouble
and surround me with songs of deliverance.

## 2 THESSALONIANS 3:3

The Lord is faithful, and he will strengthen and protect you from the evil one.

# Provision of God

**PHILIPPIANS 4:19**
My God will meet all your needs according to his glorious riches in Christ Jesus.

**PSALM 23:1**
The LORD is my shepherd, I shall not be in want.

**JOEL 2:23**
Be glad, O people of Zion,
   rejoice in the LORD your God,
for he has given you
      the autumn rains in righteousness.
He sends you abundant showers,
      both autumn and spring rains, as before.

**PSALM 111:5**
He provides food for those who fear him;
      he remembers his covenant forever.

## PSALM 132:15

I will bless her with abundant provisions;
   her poor will I satisfy with food.

## JEREMIAH 31:14

"I will satisfy the priests with abundance,
   and my people will be filled with my bounty,"
declares the LORD.

## ACTS 14:17

He has shown kindness by giving you rain from heaven and crops in their seasons; he provides you with plenty of food and fills your hearts with joy.

## 1 TIMOTHY 6:17

Command those who are rich in this present world ... to put their hope in God, who richly provides us with everything for our enjoyment.

## 2 CORINTHIANS 9:8

God is able to make all grace abound to you, so that
in all things at all times, having all that you need, you
will abound in every good work.

## 2 CORINTHIANS 12:9

He said to me, "My grace is sufficient for you, for my
power is made perfect in weakness." Therefore I will
boast all the more gladly about my weaknesses, so
that Christ's power may rest on me.

## MATTHEW 6:30-32

If that is how God clothes the grass of the field,
which is here today and tomorrow is thrown into the
fire, will he not much more clothe you, O you of little faith? So do not worry, saying, 'What shall we eat?'
or 'What shall we drink?' or 'What shall we wear?'
For the pagans run after all these things, and your
heavenly Father knows that you need them.

## MATTHEW 7:9-11

Which of you, if his son asks for bread, will give him a stone? Or if he asks for a fish, will give him a snake? If you, then, though you are evil, know how to give good gifts to your children, how much more will your Father in heaven give good gifts to those who ask him!

## ISAIAH 58:11

The LORD will guide you always;
   he will satisfy your needs in a sun-scorched land
   and will strengthen your frame.
You will be like a well-watered garden,
   like a spring whose waters never fail.

# Purification

**PSALM 51:7**

Cleanse me with hyssop, and I will be clean;
  wash me, and I will be whiter than snow.

**PSALM 51:10**

Create in me a pure heart, O God,
  and renew a steadfast spirit within me.

**ISAIAH 1:18**

"Come now, let us reason together,"
  says the LORD.
"Though your sins are like scarlet,
  they shall be as white as snow;
though they are red as crimson,
  they shall be like wool."

**EZEKIEL 36:25-27**

I will sprinkle clean water on you, and you will be clean; I will cleanse you from all your impurities and from all your idols. I will give you a new heart and put a new spirit in you; I will remove from you your heart of stone and give you a heart of flesh. And I will put my Spirit in you and move you to follow my decrees and be careful to keep my laws.

1 JOHN 1:9
If we confess our sins, he is faithful and just and will forgive us our sins and purify us from all unrighteousness.

1 JOHN 1:7
If we walk in the light, as he is in the light, we have fellowship with one another, and the blood of Jesus, his Son, purifies us from all sin.

1 CORINTHIANS 6:11
You were washed, you were sanctified, you were justified in the name of the Lord Jesus Christ and by the Spirit of our God.

HEBREWS 9:14
How much more, then, will the blood of Christ, who through the eternal Spirit offered himself unblemished to God, cleanse our consciences from acts that lead to death, so that we may serve the living God!

# Purity

**PSALM 15:1-2**

LORD, who may dwell in your sanctuary?
Who may live on your holy hill?

He whose walk is blameless
and who does what is righteous,
who speaks the truth from his heart

**PSALM 24:3-4**

Who may ascend the hill of the LORD?
Who may stand in his holy place?
He who has clean hands and a pure heart.

**MATTHEW 5:8**

Blessed are the pure in heart,

for they will see God.

**PSALM 73:1**

Surely God is good to Israel,

to those who are pure in heart.

**PROVERBS 22:11**

He who loves a pure heart and whose speech is
gracious
will have the king for his friend.

**PSALM 18:24**

The LORD has rewarded me according to my
righteousness,
according to the cleanness of my hands in his
sight.

**1 TIMOTHY 4:12**

Set an example for the believers in speech, in life, in
love, in faith and in purity.

**1 TIMOTHY 5:22**

Keep yourself pure.

**PSALM 119:9, 11**

How can a young man keep his way pure?
By living according to your word ...
I have hidden your word in my heart
that I might not sin against you.

# Pursuit

**HEBREWS 12:2-3**
Let us fix our eyes on Jesus, the author and perfecter of our faith, who for the joy set before him endured the cross, scorning its shame, and sat down at the right hand of the throne of God. Consider him who endured such opposition from sinful men, so that you will not grow weary and lose heart.

**1 TIMOTHY 4:9-10**
This is a trustworthy saying that deserves full acceptance (and for this we labor and strive), that we have put our hope in the living God, who is the Savior of all men, and especially of those who believe.

**LUKE 12:31**
Seek his kingdom, and these things will be given to you as well.

**AMOS 5:14**
Seek good, not evil,
   that you may live.

Then the LORD God Almighty will be with you,
just as you say he is.


**JEREMIAH 29:13**
You will seek me and find me when you seek me with
all your heart.


**LAMENTATIONS 3:25**
The LORD is good to those whose hope is in him,
to the one who seeks him.


**GALATIANS 6:8**
The one who sows to please the Spirit, from the Spirit
will reap eternal life.


**PSALM 14:2**
The LORD looks down from heaven
on the sons of men
to see if there are any who understand,
any who seek God.

# Quietness

**ISAIAH 30:15**
This is what the Sovereign LORD, the Holy One of
Israel, says:
> "In repentance and rest is your salvation,
> in quietness and trust is your strength,
> but you would have none of it."

**PSALM 131:2**
> I have stilled and quieted my soul;
> like a weaned child with its mother,
> like a weaned child is my soul within me.

**LAMENTATIONS 3:24-26**
> I say to myself, "The LORD is my portion;
> therefore I will wait for him.
> The LORD is good to those whose hope is in him,
> to the one who seeks him;
> it is good to wait quietly
> for the salvation of the LORD."

**PSALM 37:7**
Be still before the LORD and wait patiently for him.

## EXODUS 14:14

The LORD will fight for you; you need only to be still.

## PSALM 46:10

Be still, and know that I am God;
I will be exalted among the nations,
I will be exalted in the earth.

## JOB 6:24

Teach me, and I will be quiet;
show me where I have been wrong.

## ISAIAH 32:17

The fruit of righteousness will be peace;
the effect of righteousness will be quietness and
confidence forever.

## 1 PETER 3:4

It should be that of your inner self, the unfading
beauty of a gentle and quiet spirit, which is of great
worth in God's sight.

## 1 THESSALONIANS 4:11

Make it your ambition to lead a quiet life, to mind
your own business and to work with your hands, just
as we told you.

# Rebirth

**1 PETER 1:3**
Praise be to the God and Father of our Lord Jesus
Christ! In his great mercy he has given us new birth
into a living hope through the resurrection of Jesus
Christ from the dead.

**TITUS 3:5**
He saved us, not because of righteous things we had
done, but because of his mercy. He saved us through
the washing of rebirth and renewal by the Holy
Spirit.

**COLOSSIANS 2:13**
When you were dead in your sins and in the uncircumcision of your sinful nature, God made you alive
with Christ. He forgave us all our sins.

**JOHN 1:12-13**
Yet to all who received him, to those who believed in
his name, he gave the right to become children of

God—children born not of natural descent, nor of human decision or a husband's will, but born of God.

## JOHN 3:6

Flesh gives birth to flesh, but the Spirit gives birth to spirit.

## 1 JOHN 4:7

Dear friends, let us love one another, for love comes from God. Everyone who loves has been born of God and knows God.

## 2 CORINTHIANS 5:17

If anyone is in Christ, he is a new creation; the old has gone, the new has come!

## EZEKIEL 11:19

I will give them an undivided heart and put a new spirit in them; I will remove from them their heart of stone and give them a heart of flesh.

# Redemption

**GALATIANS 3:13**
Christ redeemed us from the curse of the law by
becoming a curse for us, for it is written: "Cursed is
everyone who is hung on a tree."

**1 PETER 1:18-19**
For you know that it was not with perishable things
such as silver or gold that you were redeemed from
the empty way of life handed down to you from your
forefathers, but with the precious blood of Christ, a
lamb without blemish or defect.

**HEBREWS 9:12**
He did not enter by means of the blood of goats and
calves; but he entered the Most Holy Place once for
all by his own blood, having obtained eternal
redemption.

**EPHESIANS 1:7**
In him we have redemption through his blood, the
forgiveness of sins, in accordance with the riches of
God's grace

## 1 CORINTHIANS 1:30

It is because of him that you are in Christ Jesus, who has become for us wisdom from God—that is, our righteousness, holiness and redemption.

## COLOSSIANS 1:13-14

For he has rescued us from the dominion of darkness and brought us into the kingdom of the Son he loves, in whom we have redemption, the forgiveness of sins.

## LAMENTATIONS 3:57-58

You came near when I called you,
and you said, "Do not fear."

O Lord, you took up my case;
you redeemed my life.

## ISAIAH 44:22

I have swept away your offenses like a cloud,
your sins like the morning mist.
Return to me,
for I have redeemed you.

# Refreshment

**ACTS 3:19**
Repent, then, and turn to God, so that your sins may
be wiped out, that times of refreshing may come from
the Lord.

**PSALM 68:9**
You gave abundant showers, O God;
you refreshed your weary inheritance.

**JEREMIAH 31:25**
I will refresh the weary and satisfy the faint.

**MATTHEW 11:28**
Come to me, all you who are weary and burdened,
and I will give you rest.

**PSALM 68:19**
Praise be to the Lord, to God our Savior,
who daily bears our burdens.

**PSALM 18:16**

He reached down from on high and took hold
of me;
he drew me out of deep waters.

**PSALM 107:6**

They cried out to the LORD in their trouble,
and he delivered them from their distress.

**REVELATION 21:4**

He will wipe every tear from their eyes. There will be
no more death or mourning or crying or pain, for the
old order of things has passed away.

**PSALM 116:8**

For you, O LORD, have delivered my soul from
death,
my eyes from tears,
my feet from stumbling.

**PHILEMON 1:20**

I do wish, brother, that I may have some benefit from
you in the Lord; refresh my heart in Christ.

# Repentance

**ACTS 2:38**
Peter replied, "Repent and be baptized, every one of you, in the name of Jesus Christ for the forgiveness of your sins. And you will receive the gift of the Holy Spirit."

**ACTS 3:19**
Repent, then, and turn to God, so that your sins may be wiped out, that times of refreshing may come from the Lord.

**ISAIAH 30:15**
This is what the Sovereign LORD, the Holy One of Israel, says:

"In repentance and rest is your salvation,

in quietness and trust is your strength,
but you would have none of it."

## 2 PETER 3:9
The Lord is not slow in keeping his promise, as some
understand slowness. He is patient with you, not
wanting anyone to perish, but everyone to come to
repentance.

## LUKE 15:7
I tell you that in the same way there will be more
rejoicing in heaven over one sinner who repents than
over ninety-nine righteous persons who do not need
to repent.

## ROMANS 2:4

Do you show contempt for the riches of his kindness, tolerance and patience, not realizing that God's kindness leads you toward repentance?

## 2 CORINTHIANS 7:10

Godly sorrow brings repentance that leads to salvation and leaves no regret, but worldly sorrow brings death.

## 2 CHRONICLES 7:14

If my people, who are called by my name, will humble themselves and pray and seek my face and turn from their wicked ways, then will I hear from heaven and will forgive their sin and will heal their land.

## EZEKIEL 18:21

If a wicked man turns away from all the sins he has committed and keeps all my decrees and does what is just and right, he will surely live; he will not die.

**ISAIAH 55:7**

Let the wicked forsake his way
and the evil man his thoughts.
Let him turn to the LORD, and he will have mercy
on him,
and to our God, for he will freely pardon.

**LUKE 5:31-32**

Jesus answered them, "It is not the healthy who need
a doctor, but the sick. I have not come to call the
righteous, but sinners to repentance."

**LUKE 15:10**

In the same way, I tell you, there is rejoicing in the
presence of the angels of God over one sinner who
repents.

# Rest

**JEREMIAH 6:16**
This is what the LORD says:
"Stand at the crossroads and look;
    ask for the ancient paths,
  ask where the good way is, and walk in it,
      and you will find rest for your souls.
      But you said, 'We will not walk in it.'"

**EXODUS 33:14**
The LORD replied, "My Presence will go with you,
and I will give you rest."

**PSALM 91:1**
  He who dwells in the shelter of the Most High
      will rest in the shadow of the Almighty.

**MATTHEW 11:28-30**
Come to me, all you who are weary and burdened,
and I will give you rest. Take my yoke upon you and
learn from me, for I am gentle and humble in heart,
and you will find rest for your souls. For my yoke is
easy and my burden is light.

**JEREMIAH 31:25**
I will refresh the weary and satisfy the faint.

**PSALM 4:8**
I will lie down and sleep in peace,
for you alone, O LORD,
make me dwell in safety.

**PSALM 62:1-2**
My soul finds rest in God alone;
my salvation comes from him.
He alone is my rock and my salvation;
he is my fortress, I will never be shaken.

**ISAIAH 32:18**
My people will live in peaceful dwelling places,
in secure homes,
in undisturbed places of rest.

**HEBREWS 4:3, 9**
Now we who have believed enter that rest, just as
God has said,
"So I declared on oath in my anger,
'They shall never enter my rest.'"

And yet his work has been finished since the creation of the world ... There remains, then, a Sabbath-
rest for the people of God.

# Restoration

**PSALM 145:14**

The LORD upholds all those who fall
and lifts up all who are bowed down.

**PSALM 71:20-21**

Though you have made me see troubles, many
and bitter,
you will restore my life again;
from the depths of the earth
you will again bring me up.
You will increase my honor
and comfort me once again.

**EZEKIEL 34:16**

I will search for the lost and bring back the strays. I
will bind up the injured and strengthen the weak, but
the sleek and the strong I will destroy. I will shepherd
the flock with justice.

**JEREMIAH 30:17**

"I will restore you to health
and heal your wounds,"
declares the LORD,
"because you are called an outcast,
Zion for whom no one cares."

## PSALM 80:3

Restore us, O God;
    make your face shine upon us,
    that we may be saved.

## ISAIAH 43:18-19

Forget the former things;
    do not dwell on the past.
See, I am doing a new thing!
    Now it springs up; do you not perceive it?
I am making a way in the desert
    and streams in the wasteland.

## 2 CORINTHIANS 5:17-18

If anyone is in Christ, he is a new creation; the old
has gone, the new has come! All this is from God,
who reconciled us to himself through Christ and gave
us the ministry of reconciliation.

## EPHESIANS 2:13

Now in Christ Jesus you who once were far away
have been brought near through the blood of Christ.

## 1 PETER 5:10

The God of all grace, who called you to his eternal
glory in Christ, after you have suffered a little while,
will himself restore you and make you strong, firm
and steadfast.

# Reward

**JEREMIAH 17:10**
> I the LORD search the heart
>     and examine the mind,
> to reward a man according to his conduct,
>     according to what his deeds deserve.

**PSALM 18:20**
> The LORD has dealt with me according to my
>     righteousness;
>         according to the cleanness of my hands he has
>         rewarded me.

**COLOSSIANS 3:23-24**
Whatever you do, work at it with all your heart, as working for the Lord, not for men, since you know that you will receive an inheritance from the Lord as a reward. It is the Lord Christ you are serving.

**JAMES 1:12**
Blessed is the man who perseveres under trial, because when he has stood the test, he will receive the crown of life that God has promised to those who love him.

**MATTHEW 6:6**
When you pray, go into your room, close the door and pray to your Father, who is unseen. Then your Father, who sees what is done in secret, will reward you.

## MATTHEW 10:42

If anyone gives even a cup of cold water to one of these little ones because he is my disciple, I tell you the truth, he will certainly not lose his reward.

## LUKE 6:35

Love your enemies, do good to them, and lend to them without expecting to get anything back. Then your reward will be great, and you will be sons of the Most High, because he is kind to the ungrateful and wicked.

## EPHESIANS 6:8

You know that the Lord will reward everyone for whatever good he does, whether he is slave or free.

## REVELATION 22:12

Behold, I am coming soon! My reward is with me, and I will give to everyone according to what he has done.

## ISAIAH 40:10

See, the Sovereign LORD comes with power,
and his arm rules for him.
See, his reward is with him,
and his recompense accompanies him.

# Righteousness

**MATTHEW 5:6**

Blessed are those who hunger and thirst for
righteousness,
for they will be filled.

**HOSEA 10:12**

Sow for yourselves righteousness,
reap the fruit of unfailing love,
and break up your unplowed ground;
for it is time to seek the LORD,
until he comes
and showers righteousness on you.

**ISAIAH 32:17**

The fruit of righteousness will be peace;
the effect of righteousness will be quietness and
confidence forever.

**PROVERBS 2:7-8**

He holds victory in store for the upright,
he is a shield to those whose walk is blameless,
for he guards the course of the just
and protects the way of his faithful ones.

**PSALM 112:6-7**

Surely he will never be shaken;
a righteous man will be remembered forever.

He will have no fear of bad news;
    his heart is steadfast, trusting in the LORD.

PSALM 37:30-31
    The mouth of the righteous man utters wisdom,
        and his tongue speaks what is just.
    The law of his God is in his heart;
        his feet do not slip.

PROVERBS 21:21
    He who pursues righteousness and love
        finds life, prosperity and honor.

JAMES 2:8
If you really keep the royal law found in Scripture,
"Love your neighbor as yourself," you are doing right.

JAMES 1:27
Religion that God our Father accepts as pure and
faultless is this: to look after orphans and widows in
their distress and to keep oneself from being polluted
by the world.

2 CORINTHIANS 9:8
God is able to make all grace abound to you, so that
in all things at all times, having all that you need, you
will abound in every good work.

# Righteousness of God

**PSALM 145:17**

The LORD is righteous in all his ways
and loving toward all he has made.

**PSALM 119:137**

Righteous are you, O LORD,
and your laws are right.

**JEREMIAH 23:5**

"The days are coming," declares the LORD,
"when I will raise up to David a righteous
Branch,
a King who will reign wisely
and do what is just and right in the land."

**REVELATION 19:11**

I saw heaven standing open and there before me was
a white horse, whose rider is called Faithful and True.
With justice he judges and makes war.

**2 CORINTHIANS 5:21**

God made him who had no sin to be sin for us,
so that in him we might become the righteousness
of God.

### 1 JOHN 2:1-2

My dear children, I write this to you so that you will not sin. But if anybody does sin, we have one who speaks to the Father in our defense—Jesus Christ, the Righteous One. He is the atoning sacrifice for our sins, and not only for ours but also for the sins of the whole world.

### ROMANS 3:22

This righteousness from God comes through faith in Jesus Christ to all who believe.

### 1 PETER 2:24

He himself bore our sins in his body on the tree, so that we might die to sins and live for righteousness; by his wounds you have been healed.

### ROMANS 5:17

For if, by the trespass of the one man, death reigned through that one man, how much more will those who receive God's abundant provision of grace and of the gift of righteousness reign in life through the one man, Jesus Christ.

### 1 CORINTHIANS 1:30

It is because of him that you are in Christ Jesus, who has become for us wisdom from God—that is, our righteousness, holiness and redemption.

# Salvation

**1 TIMOTHY 2:3-4**

God our Savior ... wants all men to be saved and to come to a knowledge of the truth.

**2 CORINTHIANS 6:2**

For he says,

"In the time of my favor I heard you,
    and in the day of salvation I helped you."

I tell you, now is the time of God's favor, now is the day of salvation.

**ROMANS 10:9**

If you confess with your mouth, "Jesus is Lord," and believe in your heart that God raised him from the dead, you will be saved.

**ACTS 10:43**

All the prophets testify about him that everyone who believes in him receives forgiveness of sins through his name.

**HEBREWS 5:9**
Once made perfect, he became the source of eternal salvation for all who obey him.

**MARK 16:16**
Whoever believes and is baptized will be saved, but whoever does not believe will be condemned.

**TITUS 3:5**
He saved us, not because of righteous things we had done, but because of his mercy. He saved us through the washing of rebirth and renewal by the Holy Spirit.

**PSALM 40:2**
He lifted me out of the slimy pit,
     out of the mud and mire;
he set my feet on a rock
     and gave me a firm place to stand.

# Satisfaction

**ECCLESIASTES 5:18**
I realized that it is good and proper for a man to eat and drink, and to find satisfaction in his toilsome labor under the sun during the few days of life God has given him—for this is his lot.

**ECCLESIASTES 2:24**
A man can do nothing better than to eat and drink and find satisfaction in his work. This too, I see, is from the hand of God.

**PSALM 103:5**
 [The LORD] satisfies your desires with good things
  so that your youth is renewed like the eagle's.

**PSALM 37:4**
 Delight yourself in the LORD
  and he will give you the desires of your heart.

**PSALM 107:8-9**
 Let them give thanks to the LORD for his
  unfailing love

and his wonderful deeds for men,
for he satisfies the thirsty
and fills the hungry with good things.

**PSALM 90:14**
Satisfy us in the morning with your unfailing love,
that we may sing for joy and be glad all our
days.

**JEREMIAH 31:25**
I will refresh the weary and satisfy the faint.

**LUKE 6:21**
Blessed are you who hunger now,
for you will be satisfied.
Blessed are you who weep now,
for you will laugh.

**PSALM 91:16**
With long life will I satisfy him
and show him my salvation.

**PSALM 132:15**
I will bless her with abundant provisions;
her poor will I satisfy with food.

# Scripture

**MATTHEW 4:4**
Jesus answered, "It is written: 'Man does not live on bread alone, but on every word that comes from the mouth of God.'"

**PSALM 19:7**
The law of the LORD is perfect,
reviving the soul.
The statutes of the LORD are trustworthy,
making wise the simple.

**ROMANS 15:4**
For everything that was written in the past was written to teach us, so that through endurance and the encouragement of the Scriptures we might have hope.

**HEBREWS 4:12**
For the word of God is living and active. Sharper than any double-edged sword, it penetrates even to dividing soul and spirit, joints and marrow; it judges the thoughts and attitudes of the heart.

**2 TIMOTHY 3:16-17**
All Scripture is God-breathed and is useful for teach-

ing, rebuking, correcting and training in righteousness, so that the man of God may be thoroughly equipped for every good work.

**JAMES 1:25**
The man who looks intently into the perfect law that gives freedom, and continues to do this, not forgetting what he has heard, but doing it—he will be blessed in what he does.

**JOSHUA 1:8**
Do not let this Book of the Law depart from your mouth; meditate on it day and night, so that you may be careful to do everything written in it. Then you will be prosperous and successful.

**DEUTERONOMY 7:12**
If you pay attention to these laws and are careful to follow them, then the LORD your God will keep his covenant of love with you, as he swore to your forefathers.

**PSALM 119:165**
Great peace have they who love your law,
and nothing can make them stumble.

# Security

**PSALM 16:5**

LORD, you have assigned me my portion and
my cup;
you have made my lot secure.

**JEREMIAH 33:6**

I will heal my people and will let them enjoy abundant peace and security.

**JOHN 10:28**

I give them eternal life, and they shall never perish;
no one can snatch them out of my hand.

**PSALM 9:10**

Those who know your name will trust in you,
for you, LORD, have never forsaken those who
seek you.

**PSALM 125:1**

Those who trust in the LORD are like Mount Zion,
which cannot be shaken but endures forever.

## PSALM 16:8

I have set the LORD always before me.
Because he is at my right hand,
I will not be shaken.

## PSALM 55:22

Cast your cares on the LORD
and he will sustain you;
he will never let the righteous fall.

## HEBREWS 13:6

We say with confidence,

"The Lord is my helper; I will not be afraid.
What can man do to me?"

## 1 PETER 3:13

Who is going to harm you if you are eager to do good?

## ROMANS 8:38-39

For I am convinced that neither death nor life, neither angels nor demons, neither the present nor the future, nor any powers, neither height nor depth, nor anything else in all creation, will be able to separate us from the love of God that is in Christ Jesus our Lord.

251

# Self-Control

**MATTHEW 16:24**
Then Jesus said to his disciples, "If anyone would come after me, he must deny himself and take up his cross and follow me."

**TITUS 2:11-12**
For the grace of God that brings salvation has appeared to all men. It teaches us to say "No" to ungodliness and worldly passions, and to live self-controlled, upright and godly lives in this present age.

**1 PETER 1:13**
Prepare your minds for action; be self-controlled; set your hope fully on the grace to be given you when Jesus Christ is revealed.

**1 PETER 4:7**
The end of all things is near. Therefore be clear minded and self-controlled so that you can pray.

**TITUS 2:2**
Teach the older men to be temperate, worthy of respect, self-controlled, and sound in faith, in love and in endurance.

## MATTHEW 26:41

Watch and pray so that you will not fall into temptation. The spirit is willing, but the body is weak.

## 1 PETER 5:8

Be self-controlled and alert. Your enemy the devil prowls around like a roaring lion looking for someone to devour.

## ROMANS 8:13

For if you live according to the sinful nature, you will die; but if by the Spirit you put to death the misdeeds of the body, you will live.

## 1 CORINTHIANS 10:13

No temptation has seized you except what is common to man. And God is faithful; he will not let you be tempted beyond what you can bear. But when you are tempted, he will also provide a way out so that you can stand up under it.

## HEBREWS 2:18

Because he himself suffered when he was tempted, he is able to help those who are being tempted.

# Self-Worth

## JEREMIAH 31:3

The LORD appeared to us in the past, saying:
"I have loved you with an everlasting love;
I have drawn you with loving-kindness."

## MATTHEW 10:29-31

Are not two sparrows sold for a penny? Yet not one of
them will fall to the ground apart from the will of
your Father. And even the very hairs of your head are
all numbered. So don't be afraid; you are worth more
than many sparrows.

## ISAIAH 43:4

Since you are precious and honored in my sight,
and because I love you,
I will give men in exchange for you,
and people in exchange for your life.

## PSALM 100:3

Know that the LORD is God.
It is he who made us, and we are his;
we are his people, the sheep of his pasture.

PSALM 139:13-14

For you created my inmost being;
you knit me together in my mother's womb.
I praise you because I am fearfully and wonderfully
made;
your works are wonderful,
I know that full well.


ISAIAH 49:15-16

Can a mother forget the baby at her breast
and have no compassion on the child she has
borne?
Though she may forget,
I will not forget you!
See, I have engraved you on the palms of my
hands;
your walls are ever before me.


EPHESIANS 1:5-6

He predestined us to be adopted as his sons through
Jesus Christ, in accordance with his pleasure and
will—to the praise of his glorious grace, which he has
freely given us in the One he loves.

# Serenity

**PSALM 46:10**

Be still, and know that I am God;
I will be exalted among the nations,
I will be exalted in the earth.

**PSALM 4:4**

In your anger do not sin;
when you are on your beds,
search your hearts and be silent.

**PSALM 89:9**

You rule over the surging sea;
when its waves mount up, you still them.

**PSALM 107:28-30**

Then they cried out to the LORD in their trouble,
and he brought them out of their distress.
He stilled the storm to a whisper;
the waves of the sea were hushed.
They were glad when it grew calm,
and he guided them to their desired haven.

**PSALM 4:8**

I will lie down and sleep in peace,
for you alone, O LORD,
make me dwell in safety.

**PSALM 23:1-2**

The LORD is my shepherd, I shall not be in want.
He makes me lie down in green pastures,
he leads me beside quiet waters.

**I CORINTHIANS 14:33**

For God is not a God of disorder but of peace.

**PROVERBS 1:33**

Whoever listens to me will live in safety
and be at ease, without fear of harm.

**I THESSALONIANS 4:11-12**

Make it your ambition to lead a quiet life, to mind
your own business and to work with your hands, just
as we told you, so that your daily life may win the
respect of outsiders and so that you will not be
dependent on anybody.

# Serving

**PSALM 34:22**

The LORD redeems his servants;
  no one will be condemned who takes refuge
    in him.

**1 CHRONICLES 28:9**

Acknowledge the God of your father, and serve him
with wholehearted devotion and with a willing mind,
for the LORD searches every heart and understands
every motive behind the thoughts. If you seek him,
he will be found by you; but if you forsake him, he
will reject you forever.

**COLOSSIANS 3:23-24**

Whatever you do, work at it with all your heart, as
working for the Lord, not for men, since you know
that you will receive an inheritance from the Lord as a
reward. It is the Lord Christ you are serving.

**ROMANS 12:11**

Keep your spiritual fervor, serving the Lord.

**EPHESIANS 6:7**
Serve wholeheartedly, as if you were serving the Lord, not men.

**1 PETER 4:11**
If anyone speaks, he should do it as one speaking the very words of God. If anyone serves, he should do it with the strength God provides, so that in all things God may be praised through Jesus Christ. To him be the glory and the power for ever and ever. Amen.

**JAMES 2:15-16**
Suppose a brother or sister is without clothes and daily food. If one of you says to him, "Go, I wish you well; keep warm and well fed," but does nothing about his physical needs, what good is it?

**JAMES 1:27**
Religion that God our Father accepts as pure and faultless is this: to look after orphans and widows in their distress and to keep oneself from being polluted by the world.

**LUKE 17:10**
You also, when you have done everything you were told to do, should say, "We are unworthy servants; we have only done our duty."

# Sincerity

**1 TIMOTHY 1:5**
The goal of this command is love, which comes from a pure heart and a good conscience and a sincere faith.

**1 JOHN 3:18**
Dear children, let us not love with words or tongue but with actions and in truth.

**JAMES 2:14, 18**
What good is it, my brothers, if a man claims to have faith but has no deeds? Can such faith save him?

But someone will say, "You have faith; I have deeds."

Show me your faith without deeds, and I will show you my faith by what I do.

**1 CORINTHIANS 5:8**
Let us keep the Festival, not with the old yeast, the yeast of malice and wickedness, but with bread without yeast, the bread of sincerity and truth.

**JOSHUA 24:14**
Now fear the LORD and serve him with all faithfulness.

## PHILIPPIANS 1:9-10

This is my prayer: that your love may abound more and more in knowledge and depth of insight, so that you may be able to discern what is best and may be pure and blameless until the day of Christ.

## HEBREWS 10:19, 22

Brothers, since we have confidence to enter the Most Holy Place by the blood of Jesus, ... let us draw near to God with a sincere heart in full assurance of faith, having our hearts sprinkled to cleanse us from a guilty conscience and having our bodies washed with pure water.

## TITUS 2:7-8

In everything set them an example by doing what is good. In your teaching show integrity, seriousness and soundness of speech that cannot be condemned, so that those who oppose you may be ashamed because they have nothing bad to say about us.

## 2 CORINTHIANS 1:12

Now this is our boast: Our conscience testifies that we have conducted ourselves in the world, and especially in our relations with you, in the holiness and sincerity that are from God. We have done so not according to worldly wisdom but according to God's grace.

# Singleness

**PSALM 68:6**

> God sets the lonely in families,
> > he leads forth the prisoners with singing;
> > but the rebellious live in a sun-scorched land.

**MATTHEW 28:20**

Surely I am with you always, to the very end of
the age.

**PSALM 73:23**

> Yet I am always with you;
> > you hold me by my right hand.

**HOSEA 2:19-20**

> I will betroth you to me forever;
> > I will betroth you in righteousness and justice,
> > in love and compassion.
> I will betroth you in faithfulness,
> > and you will acknowledge the LORD.

**ISAIAH 61:10**

> I delight greatly in the LORD;
> > my soul rejoices in my God.

For he has clothed me with garments of salvation
and arrayed me in a robe of righteousness,
as a bridegroom adorns his head like a priest,
and as a bride adorns herself with her jewels.

ISAIAH 54:5
For your Maker is your husband—
the LORD Almighty is his name—
the Holy One of Israel is your Redeemer;
he is called the God of all the earth.

1 CORINTHIANS 7:32
I would like you to be free from concern. An unmarried man is concerned about the Lord's affairs—how he can please the Lord.

1 CORINTHIANS 7:34-35
An unmarried woman or virgin is concerned about the Lord's affairs: Her aim is to be devoted to the Lord in both body and spirit. But a married woman is concerned about the affairs of this world—how she can please her husband. I am saying this for your own good, not to restrict you, but that you may live in a right way in undivided devotion to the Lord.

# Speech

**PROVERBS 21:23**

He who guards his mouth and his tongue
keeps himself from calamity.

**JAMES 3:2-3**

We all stumble in many ways. If anyone is never at
fault in what he says, he is a perfect man, able to keep
his whole body in check.

When we put bits into the mouths of horses to
make them obey us, we can turn the whole animal.

**EPHESIANS 4:29**

Do not let any unwholesome talk come out of your
mouths, but only what is helpful for building others
up according to their needs, that it may benefit those
who listen.

**PROVERBS 15:1**

A gentle answer turns away wrath.

**I PETER 4:11**

If anyone speaks, he should do it as one speaking the
very words of God. If anyone serves, he should do it

with the strength God provides, so that in all things
God may be praised through Jesus Christ. To him be
the glory and the power for ever and ever. Amen.

## PROVERBS 15:4

The tongue that brings healing is a tree of life,
but a deceitful tongue crushes the spirit.

## EPHESIANS 4:15

Speaking the truth in love, we will in all things grow
up into him who is the Head, that is, Christ.

## PROVERBS 16:24

Pleasant words are a honeycomb,
sweet to the soul and healing to the bones.

## PROVERBS 25:11

A word aptly spoken
is like apples of gold in settings of silver.

## ECCLESIASTES 9:17

The quiet words of the wise are more to be heeded
than the shouts of a ruler of fools.

# Stability

**PSALM 16:8**

I have set the LORD always before me.
Because he is at my right hand,
I will not be shaken.

**ISAIAH 54:10**

"Though the mountains be shaken
and the hills be removed,
yet my unfailing love for you will not be shaken
nor my covenant of peace be removed,"
says the LORD, who has compassion on you.

**PSALM 62:1-2**

My soul finds rest in God alone;
my salvation comes from him.
He alone is my rock and my salvation;
he is my fortress, I will never be shaken.

**PSALM 40:1-2**

I waited patiently for the LORD;
he turned to me and heard my cry.
He lifted me out of the slimy pit,
out of the mud and mire;

he set my feet on a rock
> and gave me a firm place to stand.

## JUDE 1:24-25

To him who is able to keep you from falling and to present you before his glorious presence without fault and with great joy—to the only God our Savior be glory, majesty, power and authority, through Jesus Christ our Lord, before all ages, now and forevermore! Amen.

## PSALM 119:165

> Great peace have they who love your law,
> > and nothing can make them stumble.

## PSALM 37:23-24

> If the LORD delights in a man's way,
> > he makes his steps firm;
> though he stumble, he will not fall,
> > for the LORD upholds him with his hand.

## PROVERBS 10:9

> The man of integrity walks securely,
> > but he who takes crooked paths
> > > will be found out.

## 1 JOHN 2:10

Whoever loves his brother lives in the light, and there is nothing in him to make him stumble.

# Strength

## ISAIAH 41:10

So do not fear, for I am with you;
> do not be dismayed, for I am your God.
I will strengthen you and help you;
> I will uphold you with my righteous right hand.

## PHILIPPIANS 4:13

I can do everything through him who gives me
strength.

## 2 CORINTHIANS 12:9

He said to me, "My grace is sufficient for you, for my
power is made perfect in weakness." Therefore I will
boast all the more gladly about my weaknesses, so
that Christ's power may rest on me.

## PSALM 73:26

My flesh and my heart may fail,
> but God is the strength of my heart
> and my portion forever.

## 2 SAMUEL 22:33-34

It is God who arms me with strength
> and makes my way perfect.
He makes my feet like the feet of a deer;
> he enables me to stand on the heights.

## EZEKIEL 34:16

I will search for the lost and bring back the strays. I
will bind up the injured and strengthen the weak, but
the sleek and the strong I will destroy. I will shepherd
the flock with justice.

## ISAIAH 40:29

He gives strength to the weary
> and increases the power of the weak.

PSALM 29:11

The LORD gives strength to his people;
  the LORD blesses his people with peace.


EXODUS 15:2

The LORD is my strength and my song;
  he has become my salvation.
He is my God, and I will praise him,
  my father's God, and I will exalt him.


PSALM 59:16

I will sing of your strength,
  in the morning I will sing of your love;
for you are my fortress,
  my refuge in times of trouble.


ISAIAH 40:27-31

Why do you say, O Jacob,
  and complain, O Israel,
"My way is hidden from the Lord;
  my cause is disregarded by my God"?
Do you not know?
  Have you not heard?

The LORD is the everlasting God,
    the Creator of the ends of the earth.
He will not grow tired or weary,
    and his understanding no one can fathom.
He gives strength to the weary
    and increases the power of the weak.
Even youths grow tired and weary,
    and young men stumble and fall;
but those who hope in the LORD
    will renew their strength.
They will soar on wings like eagles;
    they will run and not grow weary,
    they will walk and not be faint.

## 1 THESSALONIANS 3:13

May he strengthen your hearts so that you will be
blameless and holy in the presence of our God and
Father when our Lord Jesus comes with all his holy
ones.

## PSALM 46:1

God is our refuge and strength,
    an ever-present help in trouble.

# Success

**DEUTERONOMY 29:9**
Carefully follow the terms of this covenant, so that you may prosper in everything you do.

**1 CHRONICLES 22:13**
Then you will have success if you are careful to observe the decrees and laws that the LORD gave Moses for Israel. Be strong and courageous. Do not be afraid or discouraged.

**JOSHUA 1:7**
Be strong and very courageous. Be careful to obey all the law my servant Moses gave you; do not turn from it to the right or to the left, that you may be successful wherever you go.

**PSALM 1:2-3**
His delight is in the law of the LORD,
    and on his law he meditates day and night.
He is like a tree planted by streams of water,
    which yields its fruit in season

and whose leaf does not wither.
> Whatever he does prospers.

**PSALM 20:4**
> May he give you the desire of your heart
> > and make all your plans succeed.

**PROVERBS 15:22**
> Plans fail for lack of counsel,
> > but with many advisers they succeed.

**PROVERBS 16:3**
> Commit to the LORD whatever you do,
> > and your plans will succeed.

**ZECHARIAH 4:6**
"Not by might nor by power, but by my Spirit," says
the LORD Almighty.

# Supplication

### JOHN 15:7
If you remain in me and my words remain in you,
ask whatever you wish, and it will be given you.

### MATTHEW 21:22
If you believe, you will receive whatever you ask for in
prayer.

### MATTHEW 7:8
For everyone who asks receives; he who seeks finds;
and to him who knocks, the door will be opened.

### JOHN 16:24
Until now you have not asked for anything in my
name. Ask and you will receive, and your joy will be
complete.

### PSALM 17:6
I call on you, O God, for you will answer me;
give ear to me and hear my prayer.

## JAMES 1:5

If any of you lacks wisdom, he should ask God, who gives generously to all without finding fault, and it will be given to him.

## ROMANS 8:26

In the same way, the Spirit helps us in our weakness. We do not know what we ought to pray for, but the Spirit himself intercedes for us with groans that words cannot express.

## MATTHEW 5:44-45

I tell you: Love your enemies and pray for those who persecute you, that you may be sons of your Father in heaven.

## EPHESIANS 6:18

And pray in the Spirit on all occasions with all kinds of prayers and requests. With this in mind, be alert and always keep on praying for all the saints.

# Thankfulness

**COLOSSIANS 3:16**
Let the word of Christ dwell in you richly as you
teach and admonish one another with all wisdom,
and as you sing psalms, hymns and spiritual songs
with gratitude in your hearts to God.

**COLOSSIANS 2:6-7**
So then, just as you received Christ Jesus as Lord,
continue to live in him, rooted and built up in him,
strengthened in the faith as you were taught, and
overflowing with thankfulness.

**PSALM 107:8-9**
Let them give thanks to the LORD for his
unfailing love
and his wonderful deeds for men,
for he satisfies the thirsty
and fills the hungry with good things.

**PSALM 30:11-12**
You turned my wailing into dancing;
you removed my sackcloth and clothed me
with joy,

that my heart may sing to you and not be silent.
O LORD my God, I will give you thanks
forever.

1 CHRONICLES 16:34
Give thanks to the LORD, for he is good;
his love endures forever.

PSALM 28:7
The LORD is my strength and my shield;
my heart trusts in him, and I am helped.
My heart leaps for joy
and I will give thanks to him in song.

HEBREWS 12:28
Since we are receiving a kingdom that cannot be
shaken, let us be thankful, and so worship God
acceptably with reverence and awe.

1 THESSALONIANS 5:18
Give thanks in all circumstances, for this is God's will
for you in Christ Jesus.

# Thoughts

**PHILIPPIANS 4:8**
Finally, brothers, whatever is true, whatever is noble, whatever is right, whatever is pure, whatever is lovely, whatever is admirable—if anything is excellent or praiseworthy—think about such things.

**ROMANS 12:2**
Be transformed by the renewing of your mind. Then you will be able to test and approve what God's will is—his good, pleasing and perfect will.

**2 CORINTHIANS 10:5**
We demolish arguments and every pretension that sets itself up against the knowledge of God, and we take captive every thought to make it obedient to Christ.

**ROMANS 8:6**
The mind controlled by the Spirit is life and peace.

**PROVERBS 12:5**

The plans of the righteous are just,
but the advice of the wicked is deceitful.

**PSALM 94:11**

The LORD knows the thoughts of man;
he knows that they are futile.

**ISAIAH 26:3**

You will keep in perfect peace
him whose mind is steadfast,
because he trusts in you.

**JEREMIAH 17:10**

"I the LORD search the heart
and examine the mind,
to reward a man according to his conduct,
according to what his deeds deserve."

**MATTHEW 5:8**

Blessed are the pure in heart,
for they will see God.

# Trust

**PSALM 118:8**

It is better to take refuge in the LORD
than to trust in man.

**JOHN 14:1**

Trust in God; trust also in me.

**PSALM 40:4**

Blessed is the man
who makes the LORD his trust,
who does not look to the proud,
to those who turn aside to false gods.

**ISAIAH 30:15**

This is what the Sovereign LORD, the Holy One of
Israel, says:

"In repentance and rest is your salvation,
in quietness and trust is your strength."

**ISAIAH 28:16**

So this is what the Sovereign LORD says:

"See, I lay a stone in Zion,

a tested stone,
a precious cornerstone for a sure foundation;
the one who trusts will never be dismayed."

ISAIAH 26:3-4
You will keep in perfect peace
him whose mind is steadfast,
because he trusts in you.
Trust in the LORD forever,
for the LORD, the LORD, is the Rock eternal.

JEREMIAH 17:7-8
Blessed is the man who trusts in the LORD,
whose confidence is in him.
He will be like a tree planted by the water
that sends out its roots by the stream.
It does not fear when heat comes;
its leaves are always green.
It has no worries in a year of drought
and never fails to bear fruit.

# Truth

**PROVERBS 16:13**

Kings take pleasure in honest lips;
they value a man who speaks the truth.

**PSALM 145:18**

The LORD is near to all who call on him,
to all who call on him in truth.

**JOHN 14:6**

Jesus answered, "I am the way and the truth and the
life. No one comes to the Father except through me."

**JOHN 8:32**

You will know the truth, and the truth will set you free.

**1 JOHN 5:20**

We know also that the Son of God has come and has
given us understanding, so that we may know him
who is true. And we are in him who is true—even
in his Son Jesus Christ. He is the true God and eternal life.

## JOHN 16:13

When he, the Spirit of truth, comes, he will guide you into all truth. He will not speak on his own; he will speak only what he hears, and he will tell you what is yet to come.

## PROVERBS 23:23

Buy the truth and do not sell it;
  get wisdom, discipline and understanding.

## PSALM 119:160

All your words are true;
  all your righteous laws are eternal.

## JOSHUA 23:14

Now I am about to go the way of all the earth. You know with all your heart and soul that not one of all the good promises the LORD your God gave you has failed. Every promise has been fulfilled; not one has failed.

# Unity

**PSALM 133:1**

How good and pleasant it is
  when brothers live together in unity!

**EPHESIANS 4:4-6**

There is one body and one Spirit—one Lord, one
faith, one baptism; one God and Father of all, who is
over all and through all and in all.

**GALATIANS 3:28**

There is neither Jew nor Greek, slave nor free, male
nor female, for you are all one in Christ Jesus.

**2 CORINTHIANS 13:11**

Brothers, good-by. Aim for perfection, listen to my
appeal, be of one mind, live in peace. And the God of
love and peace will be with you.

**COLOSSIANS 2:2**

My purpose is that they may be encouraged in heart
and united in love, so that they may have the full

riches of complete understanding, in order that they may know the mystery of God, namely, Christ.

## 1 CORINTHIANS 12:13
For we were all baptized by one Spirit into one body—whether Jews or Greeks, slave or free—and we were all given the one Spirit to drink.

## 1 PETER 4:10
Each one should use whatever gift he has received to serve others, faithfully administering God's grace in its various forms.

## EPHESIANS 4:11-13
It was he who gave some to be apostles, some to be prophets, some to be evangelists, and some to be pastors and teachers, to prepare God's people for works of service, so that the body of Christ may be built up until we all reach unity in the faith and in the knowledge of the Son of God and become mature, attaining to the whole measure of the fullness of Christ.

# Victory

## 1 CORINTHIANS 15:57
Thanks be to God! He gives us the victory through our Lord Jesus Christ.

## JOHN 16:33
I have told you these things, so that in me you may have peace. In this world you will have trouble. But take heart! I have overcome the world.

## 1 JOHN 5:4-5
For everyone born of God overcomes the world. This is the victory that has overcome the world, even our faith. Who is it that overcomes the world? Only he who believes that Jesus is the Son of God.

## ROMANS 16:20
The God of peace will soon crush Satan under your feet.

The grace of our Lord Jesus be with you.

## PSALM 60:12
With God we will gain the victory,
and he will trample down our enemies.

## 1 JOHN 4:4

You, dear children, are from God and have overcome them, because the one who is in you is greater than the one who is in the world.

## ROMANS 8:37

In all these things we are more than conquerors through him who loved us.

## 1 CORINTHIANS 15:54

When the perishable has been clothed with the imperishable, and the mortal with immortality, then the saying that is written will come true: "Death has been swallowed up in victory."

## PROVERBS 2:7

He holds victory in store for the upright,
he is a shield to those whose walk is blameless.

## PROVERBS 11:14

For lack of guidance a nation falls,
but many advisers make victory sure.

# Wealth

**PROVERBS 22:2**

Rich and poor have this in common:
The LORD is the Maker of them all.

**PROVERBS 13:7**

One man pretends to be rich, yet has nothing;
another pretends to be poor, yet has great
wealth.

**DEUTERONOMY 8:18**

Remember the LORD your God, for it is he who
gives you the ability to produce wealth, and so confirms his covenant, which he swore to your forefathers, as it is today.

**1 TIMOTHY 6:7**

For we brought nothing into the world, and we can
take nothing out of it.

**PROVERBS 11:4**

Wealth is worthless in the day of wrath.

### 1 TIMOTHY 6:17-19

Command those who are rich in this present world not to be arrogant nor to put their hope in wealth, which is so uncertain, but to put their hope in God, who richly provides us with everything for our enjoyment. Command them to do good, to be rich in good deeds, and to be generous and willing to share. In this way they will lay up treasure for themselves as a firm foundation for the coming age, so that they may take hold of the life that is truly life.

### JAMES 2:5

Listen, my dear brothers: Has not God chosen those who are poor in the eyes of the world to be rich in faith and to inherit the kingdom he promised those who love him?

### PROVERBS 3:9-10

Honor the LORD with your wealth,
  with the firstfruits of all your crops;
then your barns will be filled to overflowing,
  and your vats will brim over with new wine.

### ECCLESIASTES 4:6

Better one handful with tranquillity
  than two handfuls with toil
  and chasing after the wind.

# Will of God

**1 JOHN 2:17**

The world and its desires pass away, but the man who does the will of God lives forever.

**ROMANS 12:2**

Be transformed by the renewing of your mind. Then you will be able to test and approve what God's will is—his good, pleasing and perfect will.

**EPHESIANS 1:9-10**

He made known to us the mystery of his will according to his good pleasure, which he purposed in Christ, to be put into effect when the times will have reached their fulfillment—to bring all things in heaven and on earth together under one head, even Christ.

**GALATIANS 1:3-5**

Grace and peace to you from God our Father and the Lord Jesus Christ, who gave himself for our sins to rescue us from the present evil age, according to the will of our God and Father, to whom be glory for ever and ever. Amen.

**EPHESIANS 1:11-12**
In him we were also chosen, having been predestined according to the plan of him who works out every-thing in conformity with the purpose of his will, in order that we, who were the first to hope in Christ, might be for the praise of his glory.

**JOHN 6:40**
For my Father's will is that everyone who looks to the Son and believes in him shall have eternal life, and I will raise him up at the last day.

**1 THESSALONIANS 4:3-4**
It is God's will that you should be sanctified: that you should avoid sexual immorality; that each of you should learn to control his own body in a way that is holy and honorable,

**1 PETER 2:15**
For it is God's will that by doing good you should silence the ignorant talk of foolish men.

**1 THESSALONIANS 5:16-18**
Be joyful always; pray continually; give thanks in all circumstances, for this is God's will for you in Christ Jesus.

**JAMES 4:15**
You ought to say, "If it is the Lord's will, we will live and do this or that."

# Wisdom

**PSALM 111:10**

The fear of the LORD is the beginning of wisdom;
all who follow his precepts have good
understanding.
To him belongs eternal praise.

**1 CORINTHIANS 1:25**

For the foolishness of God is wiser than man's wisdom, and the weakness of God is stronger than man's strength.

**JAMES 1:5**

If any of you lacks wisdom, he should ask God, who gives generously to all without finding fault, and it will be given to him.

**PROVERBS 4:7**

Wisdom is supreme; therefore get wisdom.
Though it cost all you have, get understanding.

**PROVERBS 24:14**

Know also that wisdom is sweet to your soul;
if you find it, there is a future hope for you,
and your hope will not be cut off.

## ECCLESIASTES 7:11-12

Wisdom, like an inheritance, is a good thing
and benefits those who see the sun.
Wisdom is a shelter
as money is a shelter,
but the advantage of knowledge is this:
that wisdom preserves the life of its possessor.

## PROVERBS 16:16

How much better to get wisdom than gold,
to choose understanding rather than silver!

## ECCLESIASTES 7:19

Wisdom makes one wise man more powerful
than ten rulers in a city.

## JAMES 3:17

The wisdom that comes from heaven is first of all
pure; then peace-loving, considerate, submissive, full
of mercy and good fruit, impartial and sincere.

## ECCLESIASTES 8:1

Who is like the wise man?
Who knows the explanation of things?
Wisdom brightens a man's face
and changes its hard appearance.

# Witnessing

**ISAIAH 52:7**

How beautiful on the mountains
     are the feet of those who bring good news,
who proclaim peace,
     who bring good tidings,
     who proclaim salvation,
who say to Zion,
     "Your God reigns!"

**MATTHEW 28:18-20**

Then Jesus came to them and said, "All authority in heaven and on earth has been given to me. Therefore go and make disciples of all nations, baptizing them in the name of the Father and of the Son and of the Holy Spirit, and teaching them to obey everything I have commanded you. And surely I am with you always, to the very end of the age."

**MARK 16:15**

He said to them, "Go into all the world and preach the good news to all creation."

## 2 CORINTHIANS 4:13

It is written: "I believed; therefore I have spoken."
With that same spirit of faith we also believe and
therefore speak.

## COLOSSIANS 1:28

We proclaim him, admonishing and teaching everyone with all wisdom, so that we may present everyone
perfect in Christ.

## 1 PETER 3:15-16

Do this with gentleness and respect, keeping a clear
conscience, so that those who speak maliciously
against your good behavior in Christ may be ashamed
of their slander.

## MATTHEW 5:16

In the same way, let your light shine before men, that
they may see your good deeds and praise your Father
in heaven.

## MATTHEW 24:14

This gospel of the kingdom will be preached in the
whole world as a testimony to all nations, and then
the end will come.

# Wives

**PROVERBS 18:22**

He who finds a wife finds what is good
and receives favor from the LORD.

**PROVERBS 31:10**

A wife of noble character who can find?
She is worth far more than rubies.

**PROVERBS 19:14**

Houses and wealth are inherited from parents,
but a prudent wife is from the LORD.

**SONG OF SONGS 4:9-10**

You have stolen my heart, my sister, my bride;
you have stolen my heart
with one glance of your eyes,
with one jewel of your necklace.
How delightful is your love, my sister, my bride!
How much more pleasing is your love than wine,
and the fragrance of your perfume than any
spice!

## 1 CORINTHIANS 7:4

The wife's body does not belong to her alone but also to her husband. In the same way, the husband's body does not belong to him alone but also to his wife.

## EPHESIANS 5:22-23

Wives, submit to your husbands as to the Lord. For the husband is the head of the wife as Christ is the head of the church, his body, of which he is the Savior.

## 1 PETER 3:5

For this is the way the holy women of the past who put their hope in God used to make themselves beautiful. They were submissive to their own husbands.

## PROVERBS 31:27-28

She watches over the affairs of her household
   and does not eat the bread of idleness.
Her children arise and call her blessed;
   her husband also, and he praises her.

# Women

## 1 TIMOTHY 2:9-10

I also want women to dress modestly, with decency
and propriety, not with braided hair or gold or pearls
or expensive clothes, but with good deeds, appropri-
ate for women who profess to worship God.

## 1 PETER 3:3-4

Your beauty should not come from outward adorn-
ment, such as braided hair and the wearing of gold
jewelry and fine clothes. Instead, it should be that of
your inner self, the unfading beauty of a gentle and
quiet spirit, which is of great worth in God's sight.

## PROVERBS 31:30

Charm is deceptive, and beauty is fleeting;
but a woman who fears the LORD is to be
praised.

## PROVERBS 11:16

A kindhearted woman gains respect,
but ruthless men gain only wealth.

**PROVERBS 31:20**

She opens her arms to the poor
and extends her hands to the needy.

**TITUS 2:3-5**

Teach the older women to be reverent in the way they live, not to be slanderers or addicted to much wine, but to teach what is good. Then they can train the younger women to love their husbands and children, to be self-controlled and pure, to be busy at home, to be kind, and to be subject to their husbands, so that no one will malign the word of God.

**PROVERBS 14:1**

The wise woman builds her house,
but with her own hands the foolish one tears
hers down.

**1 CORINTHIANS 11:3**

Now I want you to realize that the head of every man is Christ, and the head of the woman is man, and the head of Christ is God.

# Work

**1 TIMOTHY 4:9-10**
This is a trustworthy saying that deserves full acceptance (and for this we labor and strive), that we have put our hope in the living God, who is the Savior of all men, and especially of those who believe.

**1 CORINTHIANS 15:58**
My dear brothers, stand firm. Let nothing move you. Always give yourselves fully to the work of the Lord, because you know that your labor in the Lord is not in vain.

**ROMANS 12:11**
Never be lacking in zeal, but keep your spiritual fervor, serving the Lord.

**TITUS 3:14**
Our people must learn to devote themselves to doing what is good, in order that they may provide for daily necessities and not live unproductive lives.

## ECCLESIASTES 5:18

I realized that it is good and proper for a man to eat and drink, and to find satisfaction in his toilsome labor under the sun during the few days of life God has given him—for this is his lot.

## PROVERBS 13:4

Diligent hands bring wealth.

## PROVERBS 10:4

The desires of the diligent are fully satisfied.

## ECCLESIASTES 5:12

The sleep of a laborer is sweet,
    whether he eats little or much,
but the abundance of a rich man
    permits him no sleep.

## HEBREWS 4:9-10

There remains, then, a Sabbath-rest for the people of God; for anyone who enters God's rest also rests from his own work, just as God did from his.

# Worship

**1 CHRONICLES 16:25**

Great is the LORD and most worthy of praise;
he is to be feared above all gods.

**PSALM 29:2**

Ascribe to the LORD the glory due his name;
worship the LORD in the splendor of his
holiness.

**EXODUS 15:1-2**

I will sing to the LORD,
for he is highly exalted.
The horse and its rider
he has hurled into the sea.
The LORD is my strength and my song;
he has become my salvation.
He is my God, and I will praise him,
my father's God, and I will exalt him.

**PSALM 43:4**

Then will I go to the altar of God,
to God, my joy and my delight.

I will praise you with the harp,
O God, my God.

**PSALM 95:6**
Come, let us bow down in worship,
let us kneel before the LORD our Maker.

**PSALM 100:2**
Worship the LORD with gladness;
come before him with joyful songs.

**HEBREWS 12:28**
Since we are receiving a kingdom that cannot be
shaken, let us be thankful, and so worship God
acceptably with reverence and awe.

**ROMANS 12:1**
I urge you, brothers, in view of God's mercy, to offer
your bodies as living sacrifices, holy and pleasing to
God—this is your spiritual act of worship.

## MALACHI 4:2

For you who revere my name, the sun of righteousness will rise with healing in its wings. And you will go out and leap like calves released from the stall.

## JOHN 4:23-24

A time is coming and has now come when the true worshipers will worship the Father in spirit and truth, for they are the kind of worshipers the Father seeks. God is spirit, and his worshipers must worship in spirit and in truth.

## 1 KINGS 8:56-61

"Praise be to the LORD, who has given rest to his people Israel just as he promised. Not one word has failed of all the good promises he gave through his servant Moses. May the LORD our God be with us as he was with our fathers; may he never leave us nor forsake us. May he turn our hearts to him, to walk in all his ways and to keep the commands, decrees and regulations he gave our fathers. And may these words of mine, which I have prayed before the LORD, be near to the LORD our God day and night, that he

may uphold the cause of his servant and the cause of
his people Israel according to each day's need, so that
all the peoples of the earth may know that the LORD
is God and that there is no other. But your hearts
must be fully committed to the LORD our God, to
live by his decrees-and obey his commands, as at this
time."

PSALM 81:1-3

Sing for joy to God our strength;
  shout aloud to the God of Jacob!
Begin the music, strike the tambourine,
  play the melodious harp and lyre.

Sound the ram's horn at the New Moon,
  and when the moon is full, on the day of our
    Feast;

# Youth

**1 TIMOTHY 4:12**

Don't let anyone look down on you because you are young, but set an example for the believers in speech, in life, in love, in faith and in purity.

**TITUS 2:6-7**

Encourage the young men to be self-controlled. In everything set them an example by doing what is good.

**PSALM 119:9**

How can a young man keep his way pure?
By living according to your word.

**PROVERBS 6:20**

My son, keep your father's commands
and do not forsake your mother's teaching.

**PROVERBS 23:22**

Listen to your father, who gave you life,
and do not despise your mother when she
is old.

## LEVITICUS 19:32

Rise in the presence of the aged, show respect for the elderly and revere your God. I am the LORD.


## ECCLESIASTES 11:9

Be happy, young man, while you are young,
    and let your heart give you joy in the days of
        your youth.
Follow the ways of your heart
    and whatever your eyes see,
but know that for all these things
    God will bring you to judgment.


## LAMENTATIONS 3:27

It is good for a man to bear the yoke
    while he is young.


## PROVERBS 22:6

Train a child in the way he should go,
    and when he is old he will not turn from it.

# Index

# Favorite Bible Verses

_____

_____

_____

_____

_____

_____

_____

_____

_____

_____

_____

_____

_____

_____